Fatima
and
the First Saturdays

by First Saturdays for Peace

The First Saturdays®
BOOK SERIES

D1496219

In honor of the
100th Anniversary of Our Lady's Apparitions at Fatima
First Edition April 20, 2017
First Revised Edition July 16, 2019
Second Revised Edition August 6, 2021

Cover Art:
The image of Our Lady of Fatima is used with permission from the Dominican Nuns of the Perpetual Rosary at Fatima, Portugal.

Email:
info@communalfirstsaturdays.org

www.CommunalFirstSaturdays.org

ISBN: 978-1-951233-03-7

Printed in the United States of America

In reparation for the sins committed against the Immaculate Heart of Mary

Fatima and the First Saturdays

Contents

Introduction

When Our Lady first appeared at Fatima on May 13, 1917, the world was in the midst of World War I. After that, the world experienced an even greater war as Our Lady predicted, World War II. However, World War II now seems to be in the distant past for most people. Yet, the world has become even more divided than ever, even within the same country. Wars and terrorism have become the new normal. Policies have been easily embraced, which only bring us closer to World War III. Even religion and religious people are greatly divided. A greater number of people have turned away from God and the practice of religion. At the same time, the family is under attack. The family suffers from contraception, abortion, divorce, changing the meaning of marriage, being devalued, false education, corrupt laws, and the secularized state. Is there any hope for the world? Is it too late to change the direction of history? Will fallen human nature continue its fall until all is ended? It is clear that mankind is incapable of saving itself. Only God can save mankind in this life as well as for the next.

Yet, we miss the real problem. A large percentage of those who attend Mass and receive Holy Communion, do not believe in the Real Presence of Jesus, Body, Blood, Soul, and Divinity in the Holy Eucharist. Such errors of the Faith can be devastating to the Church. Nonetheless, even before this error became more manifest, there was a problem in regard to the Holy Eucharist. Problems in the world are a reflection of problems in the Church. Problems within the Church are a reflection of problems in the reception of Holy Communion. How well prepared and disposed the faithful are determines the degree to which they will receive sanctifying grace from the Blessed Sacrament. If one is not properly disposed, the state of his or her soul can become worse than before (cf. I Cor. 11:27-30).

The flow of grace and truth from the Holy Eucharist has an effect not only on the Catholic Church but also on the entire world. The proper flow of grace will convert a secular culture into a Catholic culture, just as grace and truth once converted paganism into a Catholic culture. In 1917, Our Lady came to show us the special way our practice of the Fatima message can bring the flow of grace from the Holy Eucharist in greater measure to the faithful and thus to the world. This greater flow of grace from Jesus in the Holy Eucharist can enable us to triumph over the powers of evil. Our Lady has an essential role in making this possible as we shall see.

Of course, we recognize the fact that God has provided a solution for fallen mankind. God has sent His solution. God the Father sent His only begotten Son into the world. The only begotten Son of God became man. As the Gospel says, "And the Word became flesh" (Jn. 1:14). Jesus the Word came to dwell among us and to give His life as a ransom for many. Only Jesus could pay the price for the sins of fallen mankind. When we were yet His enemies, He died for us. In this sacrifice, Jesus revealed His incomprehensible mercy and love for us. Yet, Jesus also rose from the dead and ascended to the right hand of the Father. From Heaven, Jesus mercifully pours out the Holy Spirit Who is given to us through the Sacraments for our sanctification and salvation. We are able to live all of these Mysteries anew as we participate in the Liturgy and then live them in the world. If this is the case, then why do we bring up Fatima? It seems we have all we need to be saved. On the other hand, if we have all that we need, why is the world moving away from Christ and the love of God and neighbor?

Without private revelation, we already have all that we need for our sanctification and salvation. In Jesus, all is revealed. Private revelations add nothing to what God has revealed in Jesus Christ. Saints have walked in our midst since the time of Christ without the private revelations of the 20th century. Yet, we don't say that we don't need preachers even though a preacher cannot add anything to Public Revelation. We don't say that the Pope should not write an encyclical because it adds nothing to the Public Revelation of Christ (Deposit of Faith), which closed with the death of the last Apostle. Quite the contrary, the Catholic preacher and especially the Pope, who holds the keys to Heaven, can be quite helpful in communicating and clarifying our Faith. Further, while they add nothing to the Faith, they can add to our correct understanding of the Faith. They can also make more explicit what is already contained implicitly in Public Revelation. It is also true that authentic private revelations can be a great help to our Faith and a help to our practice of the Faith (cf. Cardinal Joseph Ratzinger, *Message of Fatima*, Vatican.va). In a way, while an authentic private revelation adds nothing to the Deposit of Faith, it can add to *our* knowledge of the Faith and in a most inspiring way.

Further, an authentic and approved private revelation can also be a great help to particular times in history and in our own time. An authentic private revelation can help clarify our Faith and point us in the right direction. In fact, as the world slides further into darkness, it can become even more difficult to understand what would remedy the situation. At the same time, a greater illness often requires a stronger medicine. This stronger medicine may merely be a combination of medications we already have. Yet, consider the massive amount of Church teaching written on our Catholic Faith. There we could learn about the various medications for the soul. With these teachings and the help of the Magisterium, we are able to verify what we believe. Yet, the contents of our Faith are so vast that we cannot totally grasp them, or we may be limited in our ability to find there which remedies we need or even need right now. Where can we find in our Catholic Faith that which will provide us with a stronger medicine? It is recommended that we learn more about this in the Fatima message, which has official Church approval and contains what has already been revealed in Public Revelation. Yet, before Fatima, it may have been very difficult to identify. Accordingly, St. John Paul II said that the Fatima message is even more relevant today than when it was first given.

In her motherly love, Our Lady of Fatima offered us a period of peace and the salvation of souls if we do what she tells us (July 13, 1917). We may spend thousands of hours trying to bring peace to the world, but our efforts may obtain very little. We think we know the way to peace, but we may not. Yet, God offers us a way through Our Lady that will bring peace to the world, and yet, He is ignored. This shows that humans, like many in the Gospels, can be very slow to grasp the truth, if at all. Yet, Our Lady drew elements from the Deposit of Faith and combined them into a super remedy. We may think we are smart, but sometimes we cannot even see what is in front of our eyes. Yet, this also reminds us that the way to peace and salvation is a matter of God's mercy and grace. With God's mercy and grace, our eyes can be opened. Yet, when will that time come that the eyes of humanity will be opened?

Further, the Fatima message needs to be properly represented.

Some interpretations of the message can be misleading. Just as we need the Church's help in understanding Public Revelation, so in this book, we rely on the Church's help in properly understanding the Fatima message.

To look at the peace plan from Heaven, we will consider the actual texts written by Sr. Lucia beginning with the first signs that helped prepare the children for what would come. We will then consider the three appearances of the Angel, the six appearances of Our Lady at Fatima, and another three appearances of Our Lord, with two of these including Our Lady, to Sr. Lucia after she entered the convent. Finally, we will recall some of the texts that came even later and which reported locutions of Jesus to Sr. Lucia as well as texts with her own reflections. A commentary is presented on many of the texts to help shed further light on what they mean. We will try to explain the significance of each visit of Our Lady and that of her Son Jesus as well as the significance of His locutions. We will also try to show the wisdom of each visit and locution in relation to the message as a whole.

When possible, we will try to show how the texts relate to and support the *First Saturdays* devotion requested in reparation for the sins against the Immaculate Heart of Mary. This book attempts to shed light on the great importance of the *First Saturdays* in achieving peace in the world and the salvation of souls within the context of the Fatima message. We will also show the advantage of practicing the *First Saturdays* in a communal form as represented by the *Communal First Saturdays*. When fitting, we will also show how the texts support a communal practice of the *First Saturdays,* although the messages also allow for the private practice of the *First Saturdays*.

We will address any objections to the Church's position on the message as those arise. Also, an appendix provides a collection of the Fatima prayers and information on how to say the Rosary.

Moreover, even those who are quite familiar with the apparitions of Our Lady of Fatima will find new insights into the message throughout this book. For what lies ahead in the world a better grasp of the Fatima message is needed. This better understanding will help us to work together for the salvation of souls and the period of peace as Our Lady promised on July 13, 1917.

Finally, the world needs love, but it will only find true love by that grace, which comes from the Heart of Jesus and through the Heart of His Holy Mother and ours. However, this idea of grace coming through the Heart of Mary might seem unusual to some. Some may wonder where such an idea originates. One might wonder why we should have devotion to Our Lady. Is this in the Scripture? Before moving on to the apparitions that follow, it will be beneficial to briefly understand the presuppositions upon which this book is founded.

Yes, we can look at the Scripture as a starting point for the basis of our devotion to Our Lady. An easy way to do this is to look at the Mysteries of the Rosary and to consider the Scripture from which they come. If understood properly, these Mysteries are a compendium of the entire Bible. It should be noted that the *Communal First Saturdays* can help us to meditate on the Scriptures from which the Mysteries are derived. This is one of the ways we can more fruitfully fulfill Our Lady's request for a separate meditation on the Mysteries of the Rosary.

So, let us begin our brief explanation of the primary roots of devotion to Our Lady in the Scripture. We should know from Scripture that no one goes to the Father except through Jesus. Before we could go to the Father, He first reached out to us by sending His Son. Still, everything begins with the Father and everything ends with the Father. This is a basic truth that underlies all the Mysteries of the Rosary.

Yet, Jesus also said, "I am the Alpha and the Omega, the first and the last, the beginning and the end" (Rev. 22:13). This is true. This also indicates that Jesus is equal to the Father. Jesus is not a human person but a Divine Person with a complete human nature, together with a distinct Divine Nature. So, shouldn't we treat the Father and Son equally? We know how to reach the Father. How then do we reach Jesus? We can begin to answer this question by considering what follows.

Jesus first reached out to us in being sent by the Father. How did He come to us? Jesus came to us through one who could worthily receive Him, an Immaculate Virgin. Jesus came through the Faith and free consent of Mary in her Heart. We see this in the Gospel of Luke, chapter one, at the Annunciation of the Angel Gabriel, which is also the first mystery of the Rosary:

> [28] And he came to her and said, "Hail, full of grace, the Lord is with you!" [29] But she was greatly troubled at the saying, and considered in her mind what sort of greeting this might be. [30] And the angel said to her, "Do not be afraid, Mary, for you have found favor with God. [31] And behold, you will conceive in your womb and bear a son, and you shall call his name Jesus.
> [32] He will be great, and will be called the Son of the Most High; and the Lord God will give to him the throne of his father David, [33] and he will reign over the house of Jacob for ever; and of his kingdom there will be no end."

Unlike other mothers, Our Lady was informed about what she was specifically consenting to. She was told of the very identity of her Child and what He was to accomplish. Mary was told that He would be called the Son of the Most High, and He would fulfill the promise made to David. Our Lady was also told that Jesus would receive the throne of David and reign over His Kingdom forever (cf. Lk. 1:30-33). Hence, Our Lady was asked to consent to the eternal kingdom, the Head and the Body, the Church, the whole Christ. She is the Mother of the Lord as Elizabeth later exclaimed and the Mother of us all, called to the kingdom of God. Through her Faith and free consent, all grace came into the world in the Person of Jesus Christ.

Later, Jesus proclaimed this Spiritual Motherhood of Mary from the Cross, "Behold your Mother" (Jn. 19:27). Also, Jesus taught us to honor our father and our mother. Jesus chastised the Pharisees for thinking religion gave them an excuse for not honoring their parents (Mk. 7:9-13). We are indebted to our earthly parents for our life. Yet, we are indebted to Mary for our spiritual life by which we can be happy forever. Our debt to our Spiritual Mother is much greater than our debt to our physical mother, and is a matter of justice as well as love. It should be no surprise then when Our Lady said to Elizabeth, "all generations will call me blessed" (Lk. 1:49).

So, we can see how Jesus came to us through His Mother, because she consented on our behalf. Mary is the way Jesus came to us. The same way he traveled to us is also the best way to travel to Him. Mary wishes to join us to her Son, and through the Son, we come to the Father. We need Our Lady to intercede for us as she did at The Marriage Feast at Cana, also a Mystery of the Rosary.

Since Mary and her husband were virgins, she asked how the conception could happen.

[35] And the angel said to her,

"The Holy Spirit will come upon you,
and the power of the Most High will overshadow you;
therefore the child to be born will be called holy,
the Son of God.

[36] And behold, your kinswoman Elizabeth in her old
age has also conceived a son; and this is the sixth
month with her who was called barren. [37] For with God
nothing will be impossible." [38] And Mary said,
"Behold, I am the handmaid of the Lord; let it be to me
according to your word." And the angel departed from
her.

In these final words, Mary expressed the consent she first gave in her Heart. As St. Augustine said, "Mary conceived Jesus in her Heart before she conceived Him in her body."

In addition, St. Luke explicitly uses the term *heart* in regard to Mary in his narrative. St. Luke refers to Mary pondering and keeping all these things in her Heart after the account of the Nativity and after the Finding of the Child Jesus in the Temple, which are also two Mysteries of the Rosary.

At the visit to Elizabeth, which followed the Annunciation, Elizabeth was filled with the Holy Spirit at the very sound of Mary's voice. What did the Holy Spirit inspire Elizabeth to say? Does the Holy Spirit inspire us in this way? Elizabeth said:

Blessed are you among women, and blessed is the fruit
of your womb! [43] And why is this granted me, that the
mother of my Lord should come to me? [44] For behold,

when the voice of your greeting came to my ears, the babe in my womb leaped for joy. [45] And blessed is she who believed that there would be a fulfilment of what was spoken to her from the Lord (Lk. 1:42-45).

Anyone who wishes to pray in the Holy Spirit will honor Mary as He did through Elizabeth. So, if we know the Scripture, the Rosary can then remind us of what we need to know about Our Lady and much more. In fact, we are only beginning to tap the riches contained in the word of God. Now let us see what the Lord wants to tell us in the Fatima message and the great importance of the *First Saturdays* devotion in that message.

Fatima and the First Saturdays

The Fatima Message in Lucia's Own Words

With Commentary

There are multiple translations of the original Portuguese text of Lucia's own words regarding the Fatima message. Below are approved translations. For a complete account of the apparitions and other autobiographical material in book form, please see "Fatima in Lucia's own words," translated by the Dominican Nuns of the Perpetual Rosary, 16th edition, July 2007. Unless otherwise noted, the quoted text below is from the above book, pages 170-198.

Apparitions in 1915

Lucia's Words

Although I cannot give the exact date, it seems to me that it was 1915 that the first Apparition took place... We were just about to start praying the Rosary when I saw, poised in the air above the trees that stretched down to the valley which lay at our feet, what appeared to be a cloud in human form, whiter than snow and almost transparent... This happened on two further occasions, but on different days.

Commentary

Note that the apparitions do not yet present a particular person whether human or angelic. Rather, there is a representation of a person in human form. The form is poised in the air above the trees. Our Lady would later appear above a holmoak tree. So, these apparitions seem to be preparing the children gradually for the appearances of the Angel and Our Lady. Also, it is interesting to note that the children were about to say the Rosary whereas later in most apparitions they have already completed their prayers.

Apparitions of the Angel in 1916

The First Apparition

Lucia's Words

But I think it must have been in the spring of 1916 that the Angel appeared to us for the first time in our Loca do Cabeço… After having taken our lunch and said our prayers, we began to see, some distance off, above the trees that stretched away towards the east, a light, whiter than snow, in the form of a young man, transparent, and brighter than crystal, pierced by the rays of the sun. As he drew nearer, we could distinguish his features more and more clearly. We were surprised, absorbed, and struck dumb with amazement.

On reaching us, he said:

"Do not be afraid. I am the Angel of Peace. Pray with me."

Kneeling on the ground, he bowed down until his forehead touched the earth. Led by a supernatural impulse, we did the same, and repeated the words which we heard him say:

"My God, I believe, I adore, I hope and I love You! I ask pardon of You for those who do not believe, do not adore, do not hope and do not love You!"

Having repeated these words three times, he rose and said:

"Pray thus. The Hearts of Jesus and Mary are attentive to the voice of your supplications." Then he disappeared.

Commentary

The apparition seems to begin in a manner similar to the previous year but is not described as a cloud. Then the human like form draws closer and becomes much more distinct. The figure identifies himself as the Angel of Peace. In the midst of World War I, the Angel comes as a herald of peace. This sets the tone for the entire message of Fatima which is one that offers peace.

The Angel invited the children to pray with him. The Fatima message invites us to pray not only individually but also communally as we see here and in later apparitions as well. Later, when Our Lady comes to request the *First Saturdays* devotion including a Communion of Reparation, she does not specify that it be done either individually or communally. One may fulfill the *First Saturdays* individually or communally as far as possible. However, the most important of the practices of the *First Saturdays*, reception of Holy Communion, is essentially a communal act, as are all liturgical acts. The *Communal First Saturdays* is a Church-approved way of providing the *First Saturdays* devotion in a communal form which makes it easier for an individual and for a larger number of people to fulfill the conditions of the *First Saturdays*.

The prayer taught by the Angel expresses the greatest virtues, the three theological virtues and a fourth virtue, which pertains to the virtue of religion. Love is the greatest of these, then Hope, and then Faith. The next greatest virtue is the virtue of religion. The prayer expresses one form of that virtue, adoration. The virtue of religion is related to justice. Religion is an attempt to render God His due.

Of course, we cannot render God His due absolutely because of the inequality between the infinite Being of God and the finite being of man. Nonetheless, God may accept our offering in dependence upon the perfect sacrifice of Jesus, His Son.

Through the virtue of religion, one exercises various acts such as worship, devotion, prayer, sacrifice, reparation, adoration, praise, and thanksgiving. The prayer taught by the Angel here expresses adoration. We see also that this prayer is a form of intercession for those who do not exercise these virtues.

These virtues and acts flow from sanctifying grace and actual grace. These virtues and acts represent the means to achieve the goal of the Fatima message for the peoples of all nations. From these virtues and acts flow peace and salvation, the goal of the Fatima message. The Angel of Peace was already bringing peace. Yet, in order that these virtues may grow in us, we will need to learn more.

3

Also, the prayer was repeated three times showing that repetition can be beneficial to us and acceptable to God. We see many examples of this in Holy Scripture. Further, keep in mind that Francisco and Jacinta became saints by saying this prayer and the other Fatima prayers repeatedly. With good reason then, the *Communal First Saturdays* includes this prayer and the other Fatima prayers before the common recitation of the Rosary.

Further, we see that the Angel teaches the children to kneel and touch their foreheads to the ground. This is interesting since it is a posture not seen within the Roman Catholic Liturgy, although Catholics may practice this posture on an individual basis. On the other hand, it is a posture found within the Muslim religion as the ordinary collective practice as well as an individual one. Certainly, this prayer posture is an admirable form of adoration in itself. It is believed that various postures of the body can be quite helpful to interior prayer. Many saints, such as St. Dominic, have made use of a great variety of such postures. Yet, could it be that God is also appealing to those of the Muslim religion?

Later, Our Lady appeared at the Cova da Iria, a place in Fatima. The village of Fatima was named after a Muslim princess who married a Christian prince. The Muslim princess was named after Fatima, the daughter of Mohammed. Fatima, the Muslim princess in Portugal, became a Christian. Moreover, it has been surprising to see the huge numbers of Muslims who come to honor Our Lady of Fatima when her Pilgrim Virgin statue comes to their city. Could it be that the Muslim people will be converted to the Catholic Church through the intercession of Our Lady of Fatima? Already, by the above prayer, the Angel is praying for those who do not believe. Certainly, the conversion of the Muslim people would contribute to the realization of Our Lady's promise of peace in the world, which we will discuss later. For this we pray.

On rising, the Angel said, "Pray thus. The Hearts of Jesus and Mary are attentive to the voice of your supplications." Even though the above prayer, "My God I believe...," does not mention the Hearts of Jesus and Mary, they are attentive to the children's prayer. Not only do Jesus and Mary hear our prayers, but also no prayer is answered, no grace is given, unless it comes from the Heart of Jesus

4

through the Heart of Mary. Every grace was merited by Jesus crucified, and He came into the world through the consent of Mary. In the Person of Jesus all grace has come into the world with Our Lady's consent. It is fitting then that as our Spiritual Mother she should distribute these graces to us.

Also, in this apparition, the Angel introduced an essential theme of the Fatima message, namely, the Hearts of Jesus and Mary. Later, attention will be given to devotion to the Heart of Mary, but it is always with the understanding that these two Hearts are inseparable.

The Second Apparition

Lucia's Words

The second Apparition must have been at the height of summer... Suddenly, we saw the same Angel right beside us.

"What are you doing?" he asked. "Pray! Pray very much! The Hearts of Jesus and Mary have designs of mercy on you. Offer prayers and sacrifices constantly to the most High.

How are we to make sacrifices?" I asked.

"Make everything you can a sacrifice, and offer it to God as an act of reparation for the sins by which He is offended, and in supplication for the conversion of sinners. You will thus draw down peace upon your country. I am its Angel Guardian, the Angel of Portugal. Above all, accept and bear with submission, the suffering which the Lord will send you."

Commentary

The children didn't seem to be saying their prayers before the Angel came but seemed to have taken advantage of the siesta hours (*Fatima in Lucia's own words*, p. 162). This time the Angel appears immediately beside the children rather than coming from a distance. "What are you doing?" he asked. "Pray! Pray very much! The Hearts of Jesus and Mary have designs of mercy on you. Offer prayers and sacrifices constantly to the most High." This seems to imply that the children could be using this time to pray and make sacrifices rather than be idle. Again, we see reference to the Hearts of Jesus and Mary. "Designs of mercy" seems to imply that the Fatima message will be a gift of mercy to the children and the world. The mission of the children is a spiritual work of mercy.

Certainly, there is no greater love as a *sign* or *proof* of the intensity of one's own love than to lay down one's life for another (cf. Jn. 15:13, *Summa Theologica*, II-II, q. 124, a. 3). However, what greater *effect* can our love have than to lead a person to the truth? For a person can only love what he or she knows. Jesus is the Way, the Truth, and the Life (cf. Jn. 14:6). Through evangelization, we help people to come to know Jesus. Then, by the grace of the Holy Spirit, they should want to be united with Him. At some point, we hope they will discover that union with Jesus means to eat His Flesh and drink His Blood (cf. Jn. 6:53-56). As we shall see later, through the *First Saturdays*, we are shown a special way to try to lead the faithful to the Eucharistic Heart of Jesus. From the grace of union with the Eucharistic Heart of Jesus, the faithful can be strengthened in performing works of mercy.

It is important to note that it is not enough to just invoke the mercy of the Hearts of Jesus and Mary, but one must also be a channel of that mercy to others. As the Scripture says, "Blessed are the merciful, for they shall obtain mercy" (Mt. 5:7). Spreading the message of Fatima itself, and in particular the *First Saturdays,* represents a form of mercy that anyone can impart to others. Providing the *First Saturdays* in a communal form is itself an extraordinary work of mercy since one can reach a much larger number of the faithful.

Lucia asked, "How are we to make sacrifices?" The Angel replied, "Make everything you do a sacrifice, and offer it to God as an act of reparation for the sins by which He is offended, and in supplication for the conversion of sinners. You will thus draw down peace upon your country."

First, let us consider the words of the Angel, "Make everything you do a sacrifice." The *Catechism of the Catholic Church* considers this very idea. While the following quotation speaks of the laity in that part of the chapter specifically treating the laity, the words apply to all the faithful by reason of Baptism. The quotation was taken from *Lumen Gentium,* n. 33, as the original source.

> Hence the laity, dedicated as they are to Christ and anointed by the Holy Spirit, are marvelously called and prepared so that even richer fruits of the Spirit may be produced in them. For all their works, prayers, and apostolic undertakings, family and married life, daily work, relaxation of mind and body, if they are accomplished in the Spirit - indeed even the hardships of life if patiently born - all these become spiritual sacrifices acceptable to God through Jesus Christ. In the celebration of the Eucharist these may most fittingly be offered to the Father along with the body of the Lord. And so, worshipping everywhere by their holy actions, the laity consecrate the world itself to God, everywhere offering worship by the holiness of their lives (n. 901).

Notice that all of these actions are able to become spiritual sacrifices. The spiritual sacrifice is the interior sacrifice, and the different outward actions are the exterior sacrifice. The spiritual and interior sacrifice is the more principal sacrifice. It is an act of the virtue of religion. The exterior sacrifice, which is more sensible, is for the sake of the interior sacrifice. In this way, the acts of the body can help to inflame the soul. It is also to be noted that all of these sacrifices can be brought to the celebration of the Eucharist and there joined to the Sacrifice of Jesus Christ. Also, these sacrifices enable one to worship everywhere and, in this way, consecrate the world itself to God.

Second, the Angel said to offer sacrifices to God as an act of reparation for the sins by which God is offended. Sacrifices are only offered to God. To offer sacrifice to anyone else violates the First Commandment. For only to God do we make an offering which signifies that He is our beginning as Creator and our ultimate end by the beatific vision. One aspect of a sacrifice is that it is an act of reparation for the sins by which He is offended. Some of those sins which offend God are also against our neighbor. Sins against our neighbor require reparation. Although sacrifice is to God alone, the satisfactory (reparatory) value of our sacrifice can also be offered for sins against our neighbor. Later, we will consider one instance of this in the request for reparation to the Immaculate Heart of Mary.

As we saw above, sacrifice is also in supplication for the conversion of sinners. This means that by the sacrifices we offer to God that we hope to obtain the graces necessary for the conversion of sinners. These graces are obtained by the one mediator with the Father, Jesus Christ. Our Lady intercedes with her Son to obtain all graces for the rest of humanity on earth. All human persons can be intercessors in dependence upon the intercession of Our Lady, the "Mediatrix of all graces" (cf. *Inseg* XIX/1 (1996) 1638 (ORE 1451:5)). Among these intercessors, in the first place is St. Joseph who appeared later at Fatima. A prayer to St. Joseph is included in the *Communal First Saturdays* before the Rosary.

The Angel stated further that by making sacrifices in reparation for sin and in supplication for the conversion of sinners, we will draw down peace. Justice is a necessary condition for peace. Reparation is a form of justice. Seemingly a great deal of effort goes into achieving justice among people. This is very good and necessary but we seem to achieve very little. The problem is that we forget that justice between people depends first on justice between people and God. We can only try to achieve justice, but when we consciously depend on the perfect Sacrifice of Jesus, our efforts can become more acceptable to God. Unless we realize our dependence on the Sacrifice of Jesus, we cannot hope to obtain any justice in the world for humankind. For there can be no true justice in the world apart from the Sacrifice of Christ.

Also, if we wish to obtain justice for others, we must not forget the one to whom we owe the most after her Son, our Blessed Mother. Has she received what is just? Sadly, very few even think of the injustices that we sinners have done against our Blessed Mother. How can we solve the injustices in the world if we don't give priority to trying to repair the injustices toward Jesus and His Mother? How can we work for justice if we don't have the virtue of justice

8

ourselves? Let us recall what Simeon prophesied to Mary, "And thy own soul a sword shall pierce, that out of many hearts, thoughts may be revealed" (Lk. 2:35, *Douay Rheims*). What does the sword of injustices against Our Lady reveal about our hearts? We pray that our hearts desire to repair those injustices.

A second point is that supplication for the conversion of sinners draws down peace. This is the case because the conversion of sinners means the restoration of sanctifying grace in the soul of the sinner. The restoration of sanctifying grace means the restoration of the infused virtue of Charity as well as other virtues and gifts of the Holy Spirit. By this Charity, we are truly able to love God and neighbor. It is not a purely human form of love but one that comes down to us from Heaven. Peace is the effect of this love. It is a peace that can permeate through the entire human society and social structure.

Finally, the Angel ended by saying: "Above all, accept and bear with submission, the suffering which the Lord will send you." The Angel said "above all." Here he told us that the most important sacrifice we can offer to God is our suffering. This is said in the context of offering our own actions apart from our participation in the Mass and our reception of Holy Communion. Also, we see that offering our suffering begins with the word "accept." It is a passive action, a kind of receptivity. This receptivity is the basis of the entire spiritual life. This receptivity is exemplified by the Blessed Virgin Mary at the Annunciation of the Angel with her "Fiat," when she said "be it done to me according to thy word" (Lk. 1:38). We are called to receive the word of God, and called to desire that it be realized in us. This word also leads us to accept and bear with submission, the suffering which the Lord will send us. One can understand this as His permissive will. Such suffering crucifies the flesh and can purge the soul of sin. Through this cross, we can come to a spiritual resurrection and new life.

Again, while we may offer our sacrifices to God daily and even throughout the day, nonetheless, we bring all of these sacrifices, including our suffering, to the Sacrifice of the Mass where they are joined to the perfect sacrifice of Jesus. We have no greater opportunity to offer sacrifice to God than in the Sacrifice of the Mass.

The next apparition will at least imply this to us. Further, the *First Saturdays* reinforces the call to join ourselves to the Sacrifice of Jesus. Also, the *First Saturdays* is practiced in addition to our Sunday obligation. Without attending the Sunday Liturgy, we cannot fulfill Our Lady's request for the *First Saturdays* devotion.

The first two apparitions of the Angel have taught us the basic language of loving God and neighbor through prayer and sacrifice. We learn how God loves us and how we may return love to Him. We may now be prepared for the highest expression of prayer and sacrifice taught in the next apparition. Without realizing it, we are being prepared for that prayer and sacrifice that is at the heart of the practice of the *First Saturdays*. It is to be noted that the three children of Fatima practiced prayer and sacrifice together. Thus, the children prayed and sacrificed communally and did so frequently. Certainly, the children also prayed and sacrificed apart from one another. In any case, the *Communal First Saturdays* provides us with the opportunity to fulfill Our Lady's request together in a communal way. This adds significantly to the strength and value of our prayer and sacrifice.

Lucia's Words

Lucia continues with the following:

These words were indelibly impressed upon our minds. They were like a light which made us understand who God is, how He loves us and desires to be loved, the value of sacrifice, how pleasing it is to Him and how, on account of it, he grants the grace of conversion to sinners.

The Third Apparition

Lucia's Words

We said our Rosary there and the prayer the Angel had taught us at the first Apparition.

While we were there, the Angel appeared to us for the third time, holding a chalice in his hands, with a Host above it from which some drops of Blood were falling into the sacred vessel. Leaving the chalice and the Host suspended in the air, the Angel prostrated on the ground and repeated this prayer three times:

Commentary

Together, the children say the Rosary and the prayer they had been taught. Already the children are being prepared for the Angel's third visit. The Angel appears "holding a chalice in his hand, with a Host above it from which drops of Blood were falling into the sacred vessel." Here we see that the Holy Eucharist is the very reality for which the children were being prepared by the first two apparitions and more immediately by their communal Rosary and prayer. Again, the *Communal First Saturdays* includes the Fatima prayers and the Rosary said together by the faithful before the celebration of the Holy Eucharist.

Sr. Lucia goes on to tell us that leaving the chalice and the Host suspended in air the Angel prostrated himself and said the prayer "Most Holy Trinity..." three times.

Lucia's Words

"Most Holy Trinity, Father, Son and Holy Spirit, I adore You profoundly, and I offer You the most precious Body, Blood, Soul and Divinity of Jesus Christ, present in all the tabernacles of the world, in reparation for the outrages, sacrileges and indifference with which He Himself is offended. And, through the infinite merits of His most Sacred Heart, and the Immaculate Heart of Mary, I beg of You the conversion of poor sinners."

Commentary

The Most Holy Trinity is the beginning and end of all our actions as well as the beginning and end of the Fatima message. We speak also of the Holy Eucharist as the "source and summit" of our lives. This is true because in the Holy Eucharist we encounter Jesus, the Son of the Father, and giver of the Holy Spirit. In the person of Jesus, we encounter a Divine Person by whose Sacred

Humanity every mercy and grace come to us from the Holy Trinity.

It is of the greatest importance to believe that Jesus is really and truly present in the Holy Eucharist, in His Body, Blood, Soul, and Divinity. However, the Holy Eucharist maintains what is sensible in the bread and wine. In theology, what is sensible we call the accidents. In the Mass, the substance of Jesus becomes present, while the accidents of bread and wine remain. When we receive Jesus in Holy Communion, He is just as present in us as He was in the womb of the Virgin Mary. Even then Our Lady also could not see Him. One could say the Conception was her first Holy Communion.

In Holy Communion, we could say that Jesus comes to us in disguise, but it is Him nonetheless. Who would say that Jesus could not disguise Himself under the appearances of bread and wine? Of course, nothing is impossible for God. Yet, many Catholics do not believe the fundamental teaching of the Faith that Jesus is truly present in the Holy Eucharist. This has led to the loss of Faith and even apostasy among many Catholics.

Returning to the third apparition, we read that the Angel does not worship bread and wine but worships Jesus. As the prayer the Angel said implies, we worship Jesus present in the Mass, and in the tabernacle, as for example, during a Holy Hour.

While we may speak of different ways God is present, such as by His power and knowledge, His word, and among two or three gathered in His Name, there is no other way of Him being present that even approaches the extraordinary way He is present in the Holy Eucharist. Yet, even this exalted presence of Jesus is for the sake of communicating an increase of sanctifying grace to the souls of those who approach Him in the state of grace.

In the prayer "Most Holy Trinity..." the Angel expresses adoration toward the Holy Trinity present through the Holy Eucharist. The Angel offers to the Holy Trinity the Body, Blood, Soul, and Divinity of Jesus Christ. Jesus, our High Priest at the right hand of the Father, continually offers Himself as a Sacrifice to the Holy Trinity. In the Holy Sacrifice of the Mass the priest joins his offering of Jesus to Jesus' own offering of Himself to the Holy Trinity. Yet, the faithful also join the priest in offering Jesus to the Holy Trinity and so

12

exercise the universal priesthood given to them at Baptism. We approach the offering in praise and thanksgiving. We offer Jesus in reparation for sin and in supplication for the conversion of us sinners, a conversion which is a lifelong process.

The Angel continues the prayer "Most Holy Trinity..." by saying that the Body, Blood, Soul, and Divinity are present in all the tabernacles of the world. This is not to be understood that the Angel is only offering Jesus present in all the tabernacles of the world since the Chalice and the Host He is offering is not in a tabernacle. It may be that the prayer is calling attention to the tabernacle as the place where the Eucharist is most ignored. If we neglect the real presence of Jesus in the tabernacle, might we not lose a consciousness of the real presence of Jesus in the Holy Mass and be more attentive to other aspects of the Holy Mass? In any case, in the above prayer, when we offer the Eucharist to the Holy Trinity, we offer Him wherever He is present at that time, including in the Mass. Moreover, let us broaden our understanding of tabernacle to include the human person, who can be a greater and living tabernacle than a tabernacle made by human hands.

The prayer continues with the Angel saying that the offering is "in reparation for the outrages, sacrileges, and indifference with which He Himself is offended." Here we should call to mind the sins against Jesus in the Holy Eucharist. These sins include deliberate acts against the Eucharist, such as not believing in the Real Presence of Jesus in the Holy Eucharist, unworthy Communions, and an indifference to the Real Presence of Jesus in the Holy Eucharist. St. Paul warns us against the danger of approaching Holy Communion unworthily without discerning the Body of Christ (I Cor. 11:27-32). The *First Saturdays* brilliantly warns about and corrects those sins against the Holy Eucharist as we shall see.

The Angel then said, "Through the infinite merits of His Most Sacred Heart, and the Immaculate Heart of Mary..." One might object that only Jesus can have infinite merits because He is a Divine Person, and therefore His actions are of infinite value. Whereas, Mary is a finite person and so her actions are finite. Thus, her merits are finite. One way we might respond is to say that the prayer is not referring to the infinite merits of Mary herself. Rather, one could say that infinite merits combined with the finite merits of Our Lady are still infinite merits. Another way to answer the objection would be to consider different kinds of merit. In fact, official Church teaching has done just that. In *Ad Diem Illum* by St. Pius X we read:

> But since she surpassed all in holiness and union with Christ and has been associated with Christ in the work of Redemption, she as the expression is, merits *de congruo* what Christ merits *de condigno*, and is the principal minister in the distribution of grace.

Our Lady's association with the work of Redemption began with the mystery of the Annunciation of the Angel. In response to the Angel, the Blessed Virgin Mary freely consented to the Conception of her Son Jesus. In doing so, she consented to the infinite merits that he would gain. In a sense, we could say that she merits for us all that Christ merited but differently. Jesus merited infinitely *de condigno* or in strict justice. The Virgin Mary merits what Jesus merited but *de congruo*. *De congruo* refers to being in agreement. God found Mary's response agreeable to Himself. Also, Our Lady agreed to what God proposed, not because this was attributed to her in justice but simply from the mutual love between God and herself. Ordinarily we use the word merit in regard to justice, not love, but to have merit from God requires at least supernatural love. As we will see, the *First Saturdays* provides a way that the merited graces may flow through her to us more abundantly.

Again, the first part of the final sentence of the prayer reads: "And, through the infinite merits of His Most Sacred Heart, and the Immaculate Heart of Mary." All of Jesus' acts are the acts of a Divine Person. Thus, any of Jesus' acts have infinite merit. The infinite value of Jesus' acts as a Divine Person can pay the price for any man's sins against God. Only Jesus can pay that price to God through His Sacred Humanity which enables Him to be the one mediator between God and man. Thus, Jesus merited in strict justice (*de condigno*). The meritorious work of Jesus was completed with His Sacrifice on the Cross, which also has infinite merit. The prayer may also imply the infinite merits of the Immaculate Heart of Mary because merit (*de congruo*) here is the reward of her love that is agreeable to God as a Father. Mary's greatest merit is based on the fact that God became man by her consent. Through Our Lady's consent, we received an infinite Gift, God made man. Her consent merited the infinite, her Son, "full of grace and truth" (Jn. 1:14). Still, Our Lady's merits are totally dependent on the infinite merits of Jesus. In carrying out her Maternal role to her spiritual children, Mary is always dependent upon the merits and mediation of her Son. The result is we depend on Jesus through Mary for the graces available for our sanctification, conversion, and salvation.

The final sentence of the prayer ends with the words: "I beg of you the conversion of poor sinners." Here we can be reminded of what was said about sacrifice in the second apparition. The Angel said that sacrifice is in reparation for sin and in supplication for the conversion of sinners.

Lucia's Words

Then rising, he once more took the chalice and the Host in his hands. He gave the Host to me, and to Jacinta and Francisco he gave the contents of the chalice to drink, saying as he did so: "Take and drink the Body and Blood of Jesus Christ, horribly outraged by ungrateful men. Repair their crimes and console your God." Once again, he prostrated on the ground and repeated with us three times more, the same prayer "Most Holy Trinity....", and then disappeared.

Impelled by the power of the supernatural that enveloped us, we imitated all that the Angel had done, prostrating ourselves on the ground as he did and repeating the prayers that he said.

Commentary

After the prayer, the Angel gave the children Holy Communion. To Lucia, the Angel gave the Host only, which was the ordinary way of giving Holy Communion at the time in the Western Rite. To Francisco and Jacinta, the Angel gave the contents of the chalice only, which was not done at that time. Even now one doesn't ordinarily receive the contents of the chalice only. Possibly this signified the different paths the children were to take. For Jacinta and possibly Francisco, it was their first and last Holy Communion.

Also, one could say that Francisco and Jacinta were so well prepared by the Angel to receive Holy Communion that this one reception could be enough to make them saints.

The *First Saturdays* practiced in the communal form makes it possible to emphasize the preparation for Holy Communion. The *Communal First Saturdays* provides this by starting with the words of Jesus and Mary on December 10, 1925, followed by the intentions, especially reparation to the Immaculate Heart of Mary, then by saying prayers such as the Fatima prayers, and reciting the Rosary before Mass. In addition, the *Communal First Saturdays* proposes having Confession available before the Mass.

In addition, the *Communal First Saturdays* complements this preparation for receiving Jesus in Holy Communion by emphasizing the continued presence of Jesus afterward (cf. Pope Pius XII, *Mediator Dei*). For this reason, the *Communal First Saturdays* provides the 15-minute meditation after Mass so that the faithful can continue to be disposed to receive the graces of the Blessed Sacrament as well as try to make reparation to the Immaculate Heart of Mary (cf. Conditions of the *First Saturdays*, p. 111). Books are provided for the faithful to follow along.

In giving the children Holy Communion, the Angel said that the Body and Blood of Jesus Christ was "horribly outraged by ungrateful men. Repair their crimes and console your God." When giving the children Holy Communion, the Angel asked for reparation for the sins that offend Jesus in the Holy Eucharist. In other words, the Angel asked for a Communion of Reparation, which was first requested of St. Margaret Mary by the Sacred Heart of Jesus, especially on the *First Fridays*, and was requested again by Pope Pius XI in *Miserentissimus Redemptor*. This Encyclical by Pope Pius XI also explains how this Communion of Reparation to the Sacred Heart of Jesus can console God.

This prayer, "Most Holy Trinity…" can be offered at any time but cannot take the place of the official public prayer of the Church which bears witness that we are members of the one Body of Christ. Yet, while this prayer cannot substitute for the Liturgy, the public prayer of the Church, it could be used as a prayer to be said privately after Holy Communion as well as at other times. The children of Fatima give us an example by saying the prayer after receiving Holy Communion. Thus, the prayer helps enable us to make a Communion of Reparation to the Sacred Heart of Jesus. Later, Jesus and Mary asked for a Communion of Reparation on the *First Saturdays* for the sins against the Immaculate Heart of Mary. Thus, the same prayer could be used when making a Communion of Reparation for the sins against the Immaculate Heart of Mary.

It is to be noted that before they received a Communion of Reparation, the children prayed the Rosary, and both prayers taught by the Angel, together, and so prayed in a communal way. The children also said the second prayer, "Most Holy Trinity…" together after the Communion of Reparation. In the *Communal First Saturdays*, the faithful say Fatima prayers and the Rosary before Mass and the Communion of Reparation. After Mass, the meditation requested by Our Lady is done by the faithful together in a communal form (See CommunalFirstSaturdays.org).

Through the three visits of the Angel, the way was prepared for the visits of Our Lady in the following year for six consecutive months. During the three visits of the Angel, some basic elements of the Fatima message were disclosed. In short, the first apparition emphasized prayer and gave us a prayer, the contents of which, all prayers are meant to accomplish in some way. The second apparition explained sacrifice and how we are to make sacrifices. The third apparition showed us the ultimate realization of prayer and sacrifice to the Holy Trinity through the Holy Eucharist. In this third apparition, not only was worship expressed to God but also the desire to make reparation for sin and for the conversion of sinners. We can now examine the appearances of Our Lady at Fatima.

The Apparitions of Our Lady at Fatima and Other Occurrences

The First Three Appearances of Our Lady

The 13th of May, 1917

17

Lucia's Words

Suddenly we saw what seemed to be a flash of lightning.

"We'd better go home," I said to my cousins, "that's lightning; we may have a thunderstorm."

"Yes, indeed!" they answered.

We began to go down the slope, hurrying the sheep along towards the road. We were more or less half-way down the slope, and almost level with a large holmoak tree that stood there, when we saw another flash of lightning.

Commentary

This apparition begins with the children seeing what seems to be a flash of lightning. In order to avoid being caught in a storm, the children begin to make their way down the slope. As the children were almost level with a large holmoak tree, they saw another flash of lightning. This did not seem to be any ordinary flash of lightning since no storm followed. It is difficult to know exactly what the flash of lightning represented. It is interesting to note that "flash of lightning" occurs three times in the book of *Revelation*. One instance of the phrase in particular in the book of *Revelation* may provide a clue to the reference to a flash of lightning at the Cova da Iria. "Then God's temple in heaven was opened, and the ark of his covenant was seen within his temple; and there were flashes of lightning... And a great sign appeared in heaven, a woman clothed with the sun... (11:19, 12:1).

Tradition and various writings on the Gospel of Luke recognize that Our Lady is the fulfillment of the Ark of the Covenant. A new ark has replaced the old ark. A new covenant has replaced the old covenant. The reference in Revelation to "his covenant" can only be to the covenant that existed at the time the book of *Revelation* was written, namely, the New Covenant. Our Lady is the Ark of the New Covenant. She carried Jesus in her womb and continued to carry Him in her Immaculate Heart.

Further, we see that a woman clothed with the sun appears following the flashes of lightning in the book of *Revelation*. After mentioning the flash of lightning for the second time, Lucia told us, "... we beheld a Lady all dressed in white. She was more brilliant than the sun..." One is left to wonder if the "flash of lightning" and "more brilliant than the sun" are God's ways of further connecting Our Lady's appearances at Fatima with the woman described in the book of *Revelation*.

Lucia's Words

We had only gone a few steps further when, there before us on a small holmoak, we beheld a Lady all dressed in white. She was more brilliant than the sun, and radiated a light more clear and intense than a crystal glass filled with sparkling water, when the rays of the burning sun shine through it.

We stopped, astounded, before the Apparition. We were so close, just a few feet from her, that we were bathed in the light which surrounded her, or rather, which radiated from her. Then Our Lady spoke to us:

"Do not be afraid. I will do you no harm."

"Where are you from?"

"I am from Heaven."

"What do you want from me?"

"I have come to ask you to come here for six months in succession, on the 13th day, at this same hour. Later on, I will tell you who I am and what I want. Afterwards, I will return here yet a seventh time."

"Shall I go to Heaven too?"

"Yes, you will."

"And Jacinta?"

"She will go also."

"And Francisco?"

"He will go there too, but he must say many Rosaries."

Commentary

Our Lady tells the children that she wants them to come to the Cova for six consecutive months on the 13th of each month at the same hour, which is noon. What is the significance of the 13th and six months? At first sight it doesn't seem to have any religious significance in Christian tradition. In fact, some consider the number 13 to be an evil omen.

On the other hand, if we look back to the Old Testament and the book of *Esther*, we find the number is of great importance in the story. In fact, the number 13 appears six times in the Hebrew portion of the book of *Esther*. Recall that Esther became Queen in place of Vashti who disobeyed the King's command. Moreover, the Prime Minister, the evil Haman, was plotting to destroy all of the Jewish people because Mordecai, the guardian of Esther before she became Queen, would not bow down before him. So, Haman persuaded the King to decree that the 13th of the month of Adar would be the day on which the Jewish people would be destroyed. Fortunately, Mordecai persuaded Esther to intercede with the King and so obtained that the Jewish people could destroy their enemies on that very same day.

The above story serves to develop more fully what Our Lady is proposing at Fatima. We are being asked to do what Mordecai did, to ask that the Queen intercede with the King to bring about a triumph over the enemies of God's people. That Queen is Mary and the King is Jesus. The People of God represent the Catholic Church and those joined with her. The ultimate triumph will not be a bloody victory but a spiritual victory. The 13th of the month prefigures that day on which the triumph of the Immaculate Heart of Mary will be finally accomplished. Through the Immaculate Heart of Mary, the Eucharistic Heart of Jesus, the Lamb of God and King of kings, will reign spiritually over all nations.

It should be noted that Our Lady of the Rosary appeared at Fatima with a star on her dress. This was revealed in an interview with Lucia shortly after the apparitions. The name Esther means star.

So, this is another way that Our Lady seemed to relate her appearance to the book of *Esther*.

Further, Our Lady said she would appear a seventh time. This appearance occurred to Lucia alone at the Cova just before leaving Fatima to begin her studies in 1921 (*Fatima in Lucia's own words*, p. 175). Unlike her other appearances, there was nothing added to her message for the world. Rather, this appearance at Fatima was to console Lucia. Thus, without any further information added, it does demonstrate to us Our Lady's maternal love for each of us as individuals.

All the children are promised that they will go to Heaven. Our ultimate goal is the glory of God, but we can only fully give glory to God by going to Heaven. Heaven means to see God face to face according to St. Paul, but now we see through a glass darkly, by Faith (cf. I Cor. 13:12). Seeing God is not seeing with the eyes but rather with the intellect because the Divine Nature is pure spirit and only a spiritual faculty such as the intellect can see Him (*S.T.* p. I-II, q. 3, a. 8). Now the intellect is able to know through concepts, but for those in Heaven, God takes the place of the concept. Nonetheless, the degree of supernatural love in the will determines our place in Heaven (cf. *S.T.,* Suppl. q. 93, a. 3, St. Therese of Liseiux, *Story of a Soul*).

However, Our Lady said that Francisco must say many Rosaries before going to Heaven. The question may arise in our minds as to why Francisco is singled out as in need of saying many Rosaries. There can be no definite answer for this question. We could speculate that Francisco was not as spiritually advanced as the other two children at that time. Or, we could say that Francisco needed to do more because he would be the first one to die, a year earlier (1919) than Jacinta. Certainly, Francisco only had a short time to reach perfection. Whatever the answer, we ourselves may wonder if we too will need to say many Rosaries before we die in order to go straight to Heaven. Francisco did act upon this, for often he was found alone and secluded saying the Rosary when the children were not praying together.

Lucia's Words

Then I remembered to ask about two girls who had died

recently. They were friends of mine and used to come to my home to learn weaving with my eldest sister.

"Is Maria das Neves in heaven?"

"Yes, she is." (I think she was about 16 years old).

"And Amelia?"

"She will be in purgatory until the end of the world." (It seems to me that she was between 18 and 20 years of age).

"Are you willing to offer yourselves to God and bear all the sufferings He wills to send you, as an act of reparation for the sins by which He is offended, and of supplication for the conversion of sinners?"

"Yes, we are willing."

"Then you are going to have much to suffer, but the grace of God will be your comfort."

Commentary

Lucia asked about two of her friends who had died. It was marvelous to hear that one of them was already in Heaven. Yet, the other friend is cause for wonder. Our Lady said that she would be in Purgatory until the end of the world. Some say this meant that she would be there for a long time. Yet, this is inconsistent with what was said even if we look at the original Portuguese. Rather, it seems we could interpret Our Lady's words as conditional. Given the present state of soul of this girl, she will be in Purgatory until the end of the world. There was a case of a Sister who would not pray for those in Purgatory. It was told in a vision that her punishment was that she would not benefit from the prayers of others. Consequently, she would remain in Purgatory until the end of the world.

However, that does not exclude the possibility of others offering prayers and sacrifices in reparation for the debt that still remains for this girl since we don't her particular situation. One could especially take advantage of the indulgences offered by the Church (cf. *Manual of Indulgences*, 2006, USCCB). These indulgences can be applied to the souls in Purgatory. The plenary indulgence would especially be helpful since it offers a full remission of all debt of sin. In any case, the reality of Heaven and Purgatory has been brought to our attention. The reality of hell will be brought to our attention in Our Lady's third appearance.

Our Lady continued by asking whether the children would be willing to offer themselves to God and bear all the sufferings He wills to send them as an act of reparation for the sins by which He is offended and in petition for the conversion of sinners. This seems very similar to what the Angel had said in his second appearance except for one very significant difference. Whereas, the Angel spoke of offering everything the children did, Our Lady went further. She asked that the children offer themselves. The children themselves are to be a sacrifice, or victim souls like our crucified Savior. This offering can often mean a spiritual participation in the Cross rather than a physical or bodily participation in Christ's passion that would be out of the ordinary.

In addition, we can offer everything we do as a sacrifice, and in particular our daily duties, and especially our daily sufferings. As Jesus said, "If any man would come after me, let him deny himself and take up his cross daily and follow me" (Lk. 9:23). The grace of God will be our comfort. We will see that the theme of sacrifice is especially developed in the next two apparitions and encouraged thereafter.

Lucia's Words

As she pronounced these last words "...the grace of God will be your comfort", Our Lady opened her hands for the first time, communicating to us a light so intense that, as it streamed from her hands, its rays penetrated our hearts and the innermost depths of our souls, making us see ourselves in God. Who was that light, more clearly than we see ourselves in the best of mirrors. Then, moved by an interior impulse that was also communicated to us, we fell on our knees, repeating in our hearts:

"O most Holy Trinity, I adore You! My God, my God, I love You in the most Blessed Sacrament!"

Commentary

It is not a coincidence that when Our Lady said "the grace of God" that an intense light streamed from her hands and in a way very much similar to her apparition to St. Catherine Laboure in 1830. In this latter vision, the streaming light symbolized Our Lady's mediation of graces. Grace can penetrate our hearts and the innermost depths of our soul. As a result of such a grace, the children were able to see themselves in God. This is not Heaven or the beatific vision but it is an extraordinary mystical experience nonetheless. In any case, spiritual growth requires self-knowledge. Our greatest opportunity to acquire this self-knowledge on a regular basis is through the Sacrament of Penance. To fulfill the *First Saturdays*, Our Lady would later ask that we go to Confession at least once a month.

Self-knowledge was followed by a grace that moved the children to fall to their knees and repeat a short prayer addressed to the Holy Trinity. One is reminded of the prayer taught by the Angel at his third appearance also addressing the Holy Trinity. Like that prayer, the first act is to adore God. Yet, as a kind of abbreviation of that longer prayer in reparation for sin, the children were inspired to say a shorter prayer which expressed their love for God in the Blessed Sacrament. Yet, while this love has meritorious value, it also has satisfactory value. It is the satisfactory value of an act of love that enables us to make reparation for the sins which offend God. While this prayer is beneficial to say at any time, it could also be appropriate to say after receiving Holy Communion. It could be a part of our offering of a Communion of Reparation in the *First Saturdays* devotion.

Lucia's Words

After a few moments, Our Lady spoke again:

"Pray the Rosary every day, in order to obtain peace for the world, and the end of the war."

Then she began to rise serenely, going upwards towards the east, until she disappeared in the immensity of space. The light that surrounded her seemed to open up a path before her in the firmament, and for this reason we sometimes said that we saw Heaven opening.

Commentary

At all six of the apparitions from May to October, Our Lady said to say the Rosary every day. Promoting the *First Saturdays* helps to encourage the daily Rosary and reinforces our ability to say the Rosary better by the practice of the separate and additional meditation on the Mysteries of the Rosary. The *Communal First Saturdays* provides the best way to promote the Rosary since it demonstrates the way devotions should be directed to the Liturgy, and especially the Mass. Also, through the use of Scripture for the separate and additional meditation, one can more easily recall the Scripture related to the Mysteries when praying the Rosary with the beads. Finally, the *Communal First Saturdays* as a public practice gives visible witness on a regular basis to the importance of the Rosary in the parish, and so promotes the Rosary.

In the above passage, Our Lady said to say the Rosary to obtain peace for the world and the end of the war. Certainly, the end of the First World War did come. One could say a kind of apparent peace ensued. Yet, this was not the peace of the Gospel rooted in love of God and neighbor. One of the essential conditions for peace was greatly lacking, namely, justice. Also, Russia was going through a revolution that resulted in a Communist government, and this would result in devastating consequences throughout the world.

Then Our Lady began to rise upwards toward the east until she disappeared. This would be repeated for all six apparitions. This seems to be symbolic of Our Lady's Assumption into Heaven, which was solemnly defined as a dogma in 1950. This symbolic action establishes a close bond between Our Lady's appearance at Fatima and the dogma of her Assumption into Heaven. The Cova da Iria environment is very open so as to lend itself to any phenomena in the sky above. By comparison, we see at Lourdes, shortly after the definition of the Immaculate Conception that Our Lady appeared partly enclosed by a niche within a large cave, which could be taken to symbolize the Immaculate Conception in the womb of St. Anne. In fact, Our Lady even identified herself as the Immaculate Conception.

The 13th of June, 1917

Lucia's Words

As soon as Jacinta, Francisco and I had finished praying the Rosary, with a number of other people who were present, we saw once more the flash reflecting the light which was approaching (which we called lightning). The next moment, Our Lady was there on the holmoak, exactly the same as in May.

"What do you want of me?" I asked.

"I wish you to come here on the 13th of next month, to pray the Rosary every day, and to learn to read. Later I will tell you what I want."

Commentary

The children and some other people prepared themselves for Our Lady's appearance by saying the Rosary together. In the *Communal First Saturdays*, we say the Rosary together to prepare for Our Lord's coming in the Mass.

After the people said the Rosary, and after Our Lady appeared, Lucia asked what she wanted. After requesting the daily Rosary, the very next request of Our Lady was that Lucia should learn to read. Learning to read is essential to Lucia's mission. By reading, Sr. Lucia became very knowledgeable of Sacred Scripture. She used Scripture profusely in her book *Calls* to explain the Fatima Message. In any case, writing requires reading. It is clear that writing was a part of Lucia's mission as we see. Reading prepared her to write her memoirs and letters, and other writings as well. Later, we will show how developing a familiarity with Scripture can be a powerful aid in fulfilling the *First Saturdays* and can also help us to say the Rosary.

Lucia's Words

I asked for the cure of a sick person.

"If he is converted, he will be cured during the year."

"I would like to ask you to take us to Heaven."

"Yes. I will take Jacinta and Francisco soon. But you are to stay here some time longer. Jesus wishes to make use of you to make me known and loved. He wants to establish in the world devotion to my Immaculate Heart."*

"Am I to stay here alone?" I asked sadly.

"No, my daughter. Are you suffering a great deal? Don't lose heart. I will never forsake you. My Immaculate Heart will be your refuge and the way that will lead you to God."

*The following footnote is included with the above text: "Because she was in a hurry, Lucia omitted the end of the paragraph which, in other documents, reads as follows. "I promise salvation to those who embrace it, and those souls will be loved by God like flowers placed by me to adorn His throne" (p. 177).

Commentary

The above words of Lucia confirm that she was to remain on earth to carry out her mission. Her mission was announced in Our Lady's words as: "to make me known and loved" and "to establish in the world, devotion to my Immaculate Heart." To make Our Lady known and loved is a necessary condition before there can be any devotion to her Immaculate Heart. Love and devotion depend on knowledge. Thus, we need to know more about Our Lady's prerogatives as taught by the Magisterium of the Church as well as by the doctors and saints of the Church and those who faithfully represent these teachings to us. We need to know about Our Lady as a Virgin and Immaculate. We need to know more about her great dignity as the Mother of God and in our time more about the meaning of her Spiritual Motherhood. Our Lady began to fulfill her Spiritual Motherhood by her cooperation in our redemption. Our Lady continues to act as our Mother as our Advocate and by mediating all the graces that come to us from Her Son.

While this Spiritual Motherhood of Our Lady is already taught by the Church, a dogma concerning Our Lady as our Spiritual Mother would certainly greatly help her children to know and love her Maternal Heart better as well as provide her the special honor she deserves. One of the reasons Our Lord said the *First Saturdays* devotion is requested is to make reparation for the offenses against Our Lady's Spiritual Motherhood. We will discuss this more later.

Knowing Our Blessed Mother's love for us can help us to respond to that love. Our Lady even helps us to do this by the graces she provides. As we shall see, one of the ways we can respond to our Blessed Mother's love is by offering reparation to her Immaculate Heart for the sins against those prerogatives mentioned above.

Consecrating ourselves to the Sacred Heart of Jesus through the Immaculate Heart of Mary strengthens the foundation for our reparation to the Hearts of Jesus and Mary. For consecration to the Sacred Heart of Jesus through the Immaculate Heart of Mary is a renewal of our Baptismal consecration and vows. Not only were we anointed king and prophet but also priest which means to offer prayer and sacrifice in reparation for sin and in supplication for sinners.

These words "to establish in the world devotion to my Immaculate Heart" will be repeated again in the next apparition. This could be called the major and distinctive theme of the Fatima message. Devotion to the Immaculate Heart of Mary should not be seen as separate from the devotion to the Sacred Heart of Jesus, but should be seen as a means to make our devotion to the Sacred Heart of Jesus more complete.

Certainly, devotion to the Immaculate Heart of Mary already existed in the world at the time, so "to establish in the world" was not about starting the devotion, but about making it much more integrated into the life of the Church. Indeed, the spread of the Fatima message has certainly helped to do this, but there is much more to be done. The next apparition Our Lady will reveal two special requests for devotion to her Immaculate Heart. The fulfillment of these two special requests can lead the faithful to a more complete devotion to the Immaculate Heart of Mary, and therefore to a more complete devotion to the

Sacred Heart of Jesus. One of these requests is the *First Saturdays*. Much more remains to be done in spreading this devotion.

Next, we see that remaining alone on earth will bring great suffering to Lucia, but Our Lady reassures her that she will not forsake her but her Immaculate Heart will be her refuge and the way that leads her to God. Our Lady's Son is the one mediator between God and man, but Our Lady mediates with God through Jesus by way of His Sacred Humanity. Also, Our Lady is always dependent upon and subordinated to Jesus through His Sacred Humanity. It is the Sacred Humanity of Jesus that makes it possible for Him to be the one mediator between God and man. At the same time, the Immaculate Heart of Mary mediates between Jesus and us. Yet, Our Lady doesn't stand between us and Jesus but brings us to Jesus and Jesus to us.

Lucia's Words

As Our Lady spoke these last words, she opened her hands and for the second time, she communicated to us the rays of that same immense light. We saw ourselves in this light, as it were, immersed in God. Jacinta and Francisco seemed to be in that part of the light which rose towards Heaven, and I in that which was poured out on the earth. In front of the palm of Our Lady's right hand was a heart encircled by thorns which pierced it. We understood that this was the Immaculate Heart of Mary outraged, by the sins of humanity, and seeking reparation.

You know now, Your Excellency, what we referred to when we said that Our Lady had revealed a secret to us in June. At the time, Our Lady did not tell us to keep it secret, but we felt moved to do so by God.

Commentary

Again, Our Lady opened her hands and rays of light were communicated to the children. They saw themselves in this light, "as it were, immersed in God." Jacinta and Francisco were in that part of the light that rose to Heaven. This could mean that Jacinta and Francisco would be given the graces which would prepare them for Heaven in a short time. On the other hand, Lucia was immersed in that light which could have represented the graces that would be given to her during her long mission on earth.

The children saw Our Lady's Heart encircled by piercing thorns in front of the palm of her right hand. The children will see this pierced Heart again in the following month, and Lucia would also see it in two of three apparitions after Fatima. The children understood that the Immaculate Heart of Mary was outraged by sin and that she was seeking reparation. One should keep in mind this symbolism of seeking reparation for sin in similar manifestations that will be repeated in the third part of the secret and after the appearances at Fatima.

While making reparation is a matter of justice and it is due to both God and our neighbor when we offend them, as the Mother of God and our Spiritual Mother, reparation is due to her more than anyone else after Jesus and the other two Persons of the Holy Trinity. One of the reasons we fail in our attempts to achieve justice in the world is that we do not try to first make reparation to Jesus and His Mother. Also, if we wish to practice the spiritual and corporal works of mercy, shouldn't we first show mercy to Jesus and His Mother? Simeon had prophesied, "And thy own soul a sword shall pierce, that out of many hearts, thoughts may be revealed" (Lk. 2:35, *Douay Rheims*). It would seem that the suffering was greatest for Our Lady when Our Lord suffered and died on the Cross because of our sins. What does the suffering of our innocent immaculate Mother reveal about our hearts?

There can be no doubt while Our Lady later sought consecration to her Immaculate Heart, she emphasized reparation more than anything else in the practice of devotion to her Heart. The *First Saturdays* devotion represents the most complete practice of reparation to the Immaculate Heart of Mary. No other form of reparation can even begin to compare with the Communion of Reparation other than the Sacrifice of the Mass.

The *First Saturdays* devotion includes the Communion of Reparation together with the other supporting practices, on the day that honors Our Lady. These other supporting practices, which are

Confession, the Rosary, and the separate and additional meditation in Our Lady's company for 15-minutes, each in reparation to the Immaculate Heart of Mary, are meant to dispose the faithful to receive Holy Communion more fruitfully (cf. Conditions of the *First Saturdays*, p. 111).

Further, the *Communal First Saturdays* provides an opportunity for the faithful to practice this devotion together, more efficaciously, as a visible witness, and in an order compatible with *Marialis Cultus* (St. Paul VI). Let us be reminded of the children of Fatima who sought to pray together.

The 13th of July, 1917

Lucia's Words

A few moments after arriving at the Cova da Iria, near the holmoak, where a large number of people were praying the Rosary, we saw the flash of light once more, and a moment later Our Lady appeared on the holmoak.

"What do you want of me?" I asked.

"I want you to come here on the 13th of next month, to continue to pray the Rosary every day in honour of Our Lady of the Rosary, in order to obtain peace for the world and the end of the war, because only she can help you."

Commentary

The first words spoken by Lucia are the similar words she spoke in the two previous apparitions. "What do you want of me?" This isn't about what Lucia wants for herself but what Our Lady wants. Do we ask Our Lady this question?

Obtaining peace begins with prayer. Our Lady is speaking of the peace of the Gospel. This is a peace that flows first from the love of God and then love of neighbor. This love results from the grace of the Holy Spirit poured into our hearts. This peace is not only interior but extends from the heart out into the world bringing peace between peoples and nations.

In asking that the Rosary be said every day in honor of Our Lady of the Rosary in order to obtain peace for the world, Our Lady states that "only she can help you." Does this mean that Jesus can't help us or that the saints can't help us? No, Our Lady is totally dependent upon and subordinated to Jesus. Yet, graces can only be obtained from Jesus through her, including the grace of peace. When Our Lady freely consented to Jesus coming into the world, she thereby consented to all grace and truth coming into the world in the Person of Jesus. Our Lady has no less of a role now in Heaven. As the Scripture says, "Well done, good and faithful servant; you have been faithful over a little, I will set you over much" (Mt. 25:21). We would be denying God's word if we said that Our Blessed Mother had less of a role now in Heaven.

If Our Lady obtains all graces from her Son, then can the saints help us? Yes. However, it should be understood that the saints in Heaven depend on Our Lady when they intercede on our behalf just as they depended on her when they prayed on earth. Our dependence on our Blessed Mother is always the case whether one realizes it or not. Yet, being conscious of this dependence permits us to act more humbly and with greater efficacy.

Lucia's Words

"I would like to ask you to tell us who you are, and to work a miracle so that everybody will believe that you are appearing to us."

"Continue to come here every month. In October, I will tell you who I am and what I want, and I will perform a miracle for all to see and believe."

I then made some requests, but I cannot recall now just what they were. What I do remember is that Our Lady said it was necessary for such people to pray the Rosary in order to obtain these graces during the year. And she continued:

"Sacrifice yourselves for sinners, and say many times especially whenever you make some sacrifice: O Jesus, it is for love of You, for the conversion of sinners, and in reparation for the sins committed against the Immaculate Heart of Mary."

Commentary

Lucia asked the heavenly woman who she is, and asked her to work a miracle so that everybody would believe in the appearances. This miracle would be a stepping stone that would bring many back to Faith in God and His Church. Our Lady said she would do these things, requested by Lucia, in October and would also tell the children what she wants. The miracle will not only be a proof of the appearances but also of what Our Lady said when she appeared. Again, the emphasis in the first three appearances is on the message, reaching a high point in July. The next three appearances emphasize the proofs for the message.

In the above part of the July message, Our Lady again mentioned a more advanced spirituality of sacrifice by saying, "Sacrifice yourselves for sinners." Earlier, sacrifice was also spoken of in terms of actions and suffering. Here Our Lady speaks of sacrificing the person. In this way, we imitate Jesus who sacrificed Himself as a victim on the Cross for sinners.

Our baptismal consecration has already marked us as priests, prophets, and kings. This universal priesthood calls us to offer sacrifice as well as pray. This means that we can offer what we do, what we suffer, and our very selves for sinners. Thus, we hope to make reparation for the sins of the world as far as God enables us to do so, and to remove any obstacles to the bestowal of grace as well as actually obtain that grace.

Our Lady then gave the children a prayer to say often and whenever they make a sacrifice. The prayer begins, "O Jesus, it is for love of you." The theological virtues are the greatest of all the virtues. These are Faith, Hope, and Charity (Love), with the latter providing the motive for this prayer. Without Faith there can be no Hope, and without Hope there can be no Love, but the greatest of these is Love (cf. I Cor. 13:13). The virtue of Love is manifested in the act of

Love of God first and then of our neighbor. Love is also the mother of all the virtues and their acts. The act of Love provides the motive for all the other virtues and acts.

Further, the greater the act of Love, the greater is the meritorious and satisfactory (reparational) value of the act. Love is the motive for making a sacrifice and for the practice of all virtues. Without love, the other virtues are nothing of any lasting value. Thus, the prayer above expresses that out of love, one can offer sacrifice, an act of the virtue of religion. That sacrifice can be motivated by an act of love, love for Jesus, Who is both God and man. This act of love can console Him and provide Him reparation for the sins that offend Him.

Next, we see that the prayer offers the sacrifice for the conversion of sinners. The grace of conversion is necessary for peace in the world and the salvation of souls. Conversion may mean coming to the fullness of participation as a member in the Body of Christ by becoming a Catholic, or it could mean coming into and progressing in the state of sanctifying grace and Charity. All are called to continual conversion.

In the last part of the prayer, we offer the sacrifice to Jesus "in reparation for the sins committed against the Immaculate Heart of Mary." This corresponds with the request for reparation to the Immaculate Heart of Mary in the second apparition of Our Lady. This prayer means that we would offer all of our sacrifices in reparation to the Immaculate Heart of Mary. This prayer can also be used privately when receiving a Communion of Reparation on the *First Saturdays* or on other days. Also, the prayer taught by Our Lady doesn't prevent other intentions being added as Jacinta did.

Keep in mind that reparation to the Immaculate Heart of Mary is a more complete reparation to the Sacred Heart of Jesus. Pope Pius XII told us that our Blessed Mother was among the three greatest gifts of the love of the Sacred Heart of Jesus for us (*Haurietis Aquas*, n. 69-72). The first is Jesus Himself in the Holy Eucharist and then Our Lady. The Sacred Heart of Jesus is offended when we offend His gifts. The Angel had already taught the children the Communion of Reparation to the Sacred Heart of Jesus for sins against the Holy

Eucharist, which is the greatest of the gifts of His Heart. Yet, reparation to the Immaculate Heart of Mary opens the way to the Holy Eucharist and opens the way for the graces of the Holy Eucharist to come to us.

The third gift of the Sacred Heart of Jesus is the priesthood. Remember, the fullness of the ministerial priesthood is in the bishops. A man is ordained a presbyter (presbyteroi in Greek) who has a threefold ministry as priest, prophet, and king. A priest is one who mediates with God on behalf of others by prayer and sacrifice. The ordained priest is able to provide mediation on behalf of the people, especially through the sacramental ministry of the Church.

Yet, there is more because the presbyter has the prophetic ministry as well, and for the bishops this can include participation in the Magisterium of the Church, whether extraordinary or ordinary in its teaching. This gift of the Sacred Heart of Jesus is thus able to protect our Faith from error and guide us to a correct understanding of our Faith.

Finally, there is the kingly role of the presbyter. The king rules. The Church has laws by which it is governed. There are many kinds of laws, Divine Law, Natural Law (as exemplified by the ten commandments), liturgical law, and canon law. These laws are for the protection and benefit of the faithful. Above all, is the law of love of God and then our neighbor. So, in his kingly role, the ordained priest should lead and guide us in the way we should practice our Faith and receive the sacraments. This guidance can be found in documents, such as the *Catechism of the Catholic Church*, canon law, liturgical law, and other writings. As we shall see, the gift of the priesthood (presbyterate) plays an important and essential part in the Fatima message.

Lucia's Words

As Our Lady spoke these last words, she opened her hands once more, as she had done during the two previous months. The rays of light seemed to penetrate the earth, and we saw as it were a sea of fire. Plunged in this fire were demons and souls in human form, like transparent burning embers, all blackened or burnished

35

bronze, floating about in the conflagration, now raised into the air by the flames that issued from within themselves together with great clouds of smoke now falling back on every side like sparks in huge fires, without weight or equilibrium, amid shrieks and groans of pain and despair, which horrified us and made us tremble with fear. (It must have been this sight which caused me to cry out, as people say they heard me). The demons could be distinguished by their terrifying and repellent likeness to frightful and unknown animals, black and transparent like burning coals.

Commentary

This part of the apparition represents the first part of the Fatima secret. Why would Our Lady show these young children such a horrifying scene as this? This seems to go against our contemporary way of thinking. Yet, our contemporary way of thinking is rooted in godlessness. Secular child psychology ignores Faith and original sin. This means that children can be taught a very narrow-minded view of reality. At the same time, secular entertainment offers a pointless abundance of fictional horror.

Yet, hell shows us a very real horror where real people go. It is obvious that we should not want to go there. Nor should we want anyone else to go there. If we were planning on a hike through a wilderness area but were told there is a bottomless pit somewhere there that is easily overlooked or not seen, wouldn't we want to know more about it so that we might avoid it? Nonetheless, it can make a difference as to who tells us about hell and the way they explain it. One must speak out of love, not anger. Also, one must estimate the readiness of the person and especially the child.

Indeed, the children of Fatima were well prepared by previous appearances and graces to see hell. Not only did the Angel and Our Lady appear to them previously, and they practiced an intense prayer life, but Our Lady also promised them Heaven. This promise removed from them the greatest fear one could have in regard to hell. Yet, actually seeing hell was still terrifying. Clearly, children ordinarily would not be prepared for such a vision nor would they be shown such a vision in that case. Even adults would not ordinarily be prepared to see such a vision. We may not learn about hell by actually seeing it as did the children of Fatima. Even if we have an adequate knowledge of hell, we ordinarily learn about it in a much less frightening way than did the children.

What effect did the vision of hell have on the children? As one might expect, the youngest child, Jacinta, was the most frightened by what she saw. Yet, ironically, the vision seemed to make the biggest impression on her than on the other children, while the other children seemed to emphasize other aspects of the message. Because of the vision of hell, it was Jacinta who greatly enlarged her love for those in danger of perdition. It was Jacinta more than the others who sought to make sacrifices for souls so that they would not go to hell. Jacinta can teach us that we often lose sight of what the knowledge of hell is meant to accomplish. Certainly, there can be a value to servile fear in the beginning of the spiritual life as a disposition for our own salvation, but the awareness of hell should lead to something much greater. The teaching on hell is meant to help increase our love for others. On the other hand, when hell is excluded from consideration, are we as motivated to sacrifice ourselves for the salvation of others? It seems we are not so motivated to sacrifice ourselves for the salvation of others. It is unfortunate for so many to be deprived of this greater motivation in loving our neighbor. It is also a great tragedy for souls when hell is not taught in the way Jesus taught it. Too often many overlook the reality of hell and the other names for it, even though it appears repeatedly in the Gospel readings. We should keep in mind what St. Faustina told us about her vision of hell. She said that "most of the souls there are those who disbelieved that there is a hell" (*Diary* of St. Faustina, n. 741).

Lucia's Words

Terrified and as if to plead for succour, we looked up at Our Lady, who said to us, so kindly and so sadly:

"You have seen hell where the souls of poor sinners go. To save them, God wishes to establish in the world devotion to my Immaculate Heart. If what I say to you is done, many souls will be saved and there will be peace. The war is going to end; but if people do not cease offending God, a worse one will break out during the pontificate of Pius XI. When you see a night illumined by an unknown light, know that this is the great sign given you by God that He is about to punish the world for its crimes, by means of war, famine, and persecutions of the Church and of the Holy Father.

Commentary

Terrified by what they saw, the children were told by Our Lady that they had seen hell where poor sinners go. This is a loving act of the Immaculate Heart of Mary, to warn the children about this place where sinners go. Yet, the children were already told that they were going to Heaven. What then is the purpose of showing the children a vision of hell? In a sense, Our Lady was saying that there are consequences to our actions. Our Lady wished to stir up love for their neighbor and especially for those who were on their way to hell. Subsequently, the children greatly increased their love for others, praying and sacrificing all the more that others would be saved from eternal punishment. Helping to save souls is the greatest act of Charity to others, especially through the gift of truth. Otherwise, if hell did not exist and everyone went to Heaven for all eternity, where would be the urgency to act or even the need to do anything?

What must be done to save so many souls that are on the path to hell? From the beginning of Christianity, we have been provided with all that is needed to be saved from hell. Yet, this doesn't always mean that we are conscious of all that has been revealed for our salvation. We may emphasize some elements of Public Revelation more than others which may also need attention. There are also things which are contained in Public Revelation that may have not been made explicit and which can be of help. Further, the particular times in which we live may make it especially difficult to retain our Faith. Also, Jesus formed us into a body in which we are mutually interdependent on one another. Yet, it is also possible in certain times more than others not to be able to get the help we need from one another. Confusion can even enter into the Body of Christ, making it difficult for its members to see clearly.

A private revelation does not add anything new to the Public Revelation made by Jesus Christ to the Church. Even the Magisterium of the Church does not add anything to Public Revelation, also known as the *Deposit of Faith*. Yet, the Magisterium of the Church is essential to the correct explanation of that Revelation. Nonetheless, a private revelation officially approved by the authority of the Church can be of great help in all of the above problems facing the faithful. In fact, an approved apparition can direct us to see what is being overlooked in the complete understanding of the Deposit of Faith. Otherwise, we may lose the proper focus and begin to drift away from the right path.

The appearances of the Sacred Heart of Jesus to St. Margaret Mary in the 17th century emphasized His love for us and that He is greatly offended by our sins, especially those against the Holy Eucharist. Jesus asked for devotion to His Sacred Heart and in particular for a Communion of Reparation on the *First Fridays* in reparation to His Heart. Remember, the Holy Eucharist, in which Jesus is really present, is the greatest gift of His Sacred Heart to us.

Our times are increasingly without a sense of God and sin, and so we need more help to survive the spiritually toxic environment in which we live. We need to make our devotion to the Sacred Heart of Jesus more complete. Our Lady told the children that to save souls from hell, "God wishes to establish in the world devotion to My Immaculate Heart." This devotion is not meant to compete with devotion to the Sacred Heart of Jesus. Quite the contrary, through devotion to her Immaculate Heart, Our Lady wishes to join us to the Sacred Heart of Jesus. Also, as mentioned above, the Immaculate Heart of Mary is one of the three greatest gifts of the Sacred Heart of Jesus to us (Pope Pius XII, *Aquas Haurietis*). Not to receive this gift of Jesus' Mother with devotion is to offend His Sacred Heart.

If we did what Our Lady told us, she said there would be peace. Our Lady said that the war (World War I) was about to end but if people did not cease offending God, a worse one would occur during the reign of Pope Pius XI.

Pope Pius XI died on February 10, 1939. It might seem that this is before the war since the gunfire began September 1, 1939 with the invasion of Poland by Nazi Germany. However, Sr. Lucia believed that the war actually began earlier beginning with the annexation of Austria as German troops marched across the border without a shot being fired. This occurred on March 12, 1938. Later, in September of the same year, Nazi Germany annexed a part of Czechoslovakia called the Sudetenland. German troops simply occupied the Sudetenland without firing a shot. This was made possible by the Munich Agreement. Four powers signed, Britain, France, Italy, and Germany. Czechoslovakia was not invited. Since Britain and France had been allies of Czechoslovakia, one can see this was a great betrayal. The Prime Minister of Britain, Neville Chamberlain returned from the agreement and said, "Peace in our time."

Yet, Winston Churchill sharply criticized the Munich Agreement and said it meant war and not peace. Thus, the way was paved for World War II. An immoral agreement cannot bring peace. However, there can be peace if we do what Our Lady asks us to do. So, it is a mystery that even good people look elsewhere for peace.

Our Lady foretold a great sign that tragic events would follow, "When you see a night illumined by an unknown light, know that this is the great sign given you by God that He is about to punish the world for its crimes, by means of war, famine and persecutions of the Church and of the Holy Father." Sr. Lucia believed that this unknown light took place on January 25-26, 1938 (cf. *Fatima in Lucia's own words*, p. 179). Others said that the sky lit up throughout the world. Some thought it was an aurora borealis, but nothing this intensive and extensive had been seen as far as anyone could remember or had heard of. It was as if the sky was on fire. Something like curtains of fire could be seen on the horizon that made it appear that a city was on fire. Fire trucks would go to and fro but not find any fires (cf. *New York Times*, January 26, 1938, LE, p. 25).

In any case, the greatest war in history did follow the unknown light. The war actually began when German troops marched into Austria without justification or provocation on March 12, 1938 and before the death of Pope Pius XI. The fulfillment of the other prophecies also followed. Not only that, but the Communist Soviet Union (USSR) eventually gained control of many countries in Eastern Europe, including East Germany. Also, not many years after the war,

China came under Communist rule. In addition, the errors of Russia, which is Communism, had spread throughout the world.

Lucia's Words

"To prevent this, I shall come to ask for the consecration of Russia to my Immaculate Heart, and the Communion of Reparation on the First Saturdays. If my requests are heeded, Russia will be converted, and there will be peace; if not, she will spread her errors throughout the world, causing wars and persecutions of the Church. The good will be martyred, the Holy Father will have much to suffer, various nations will be annihilated. In the end, my Immaculate Heart will triumph. The Holy Father will consecrate Russia to me and she will be converted, and a period of peace will be granted to the world."

Commentary

Returning to the third appearance of Our Lady, we still need to review what Our Lady wants us to do in order to establish devotion to her Immaculate Heart. As a solution for the war and the other punishments, Our Lady said, "To prevent this, I shall come to ask for the consecration of Russia to My Immaculate Heart, and the Communion of Reparation on the first Saturdays."

Besides practicing devotion to the Immaculate Heart of Mary on a daily basis, Our Lady told of these two special requests that she said she would come to ask for later. Our Lady would come to ask for these two special requests later so that they could be revealed apart from the secret and at the appropriate time. The separate revelation of these two requests later allowed Lucia to make them known. Also, while the secret provided the children some idea as to what the two special requests would be and allowed the children to discuss the two requests among themselves, Lucia would still need a further explanation as to how these two requests should be fulfilled. All of this will become clearer when we examine the post Fatima apparitions.

Our Lady continued and said, "If my requests are heeded, Russia will be converted, and there will be peace; if not, she will spread her errors throughout the world, causing wars and persecutions of the Church." Our Lady said, "my requests," not my request. It has been falsely said that the consecration of Russia is all that is necessary for its conversion and peace. Yet, we can see that both requests must be fulfilled. The Pope and the bishops did their part in making the consecration on March 25, 1984.

The People of God must do their part as well in fulfilling the second request through the practice of the *First Saturdays*. Peace and the conversion of nations are only possible if the people are sanctified, and this begins with the Catholic Church. The *First Saturdays* devotion has been designed by Heaven to show us how to bring this about.

Also, the focus on the consecration of Russia, as the sole means of its complete conversion, overlooks the secret on July 13, 1917 and Our Lord's locutions to Lucia during the 1930s. While not referring to a conversion, Our Lord did tell Lucia that when the consecration of Russia was fulfilled the persecution would stop. The promise of the end of persecution implied that there would be religious freedom again (See below, Letters and Locutions, May 29, 1930, p. 99). (Jesus did not say that fulfilling the first request was sufficient to bring about the complete conversion of Russia). In fact, not long after the collegial act of consecration on March 25, 1984, the Soviet Union began to collapse and the religious persecution gave way to greater religious freedom. Since the fall of the Soviet Union until at least 2021, the practice of Christianity has continued to grow in Russia while it is decreasing in the West.

Further, the notion that this consecration alone is necessary to bring about the complete conversion of Russia appears to conflict with theology as well as with Our Lady's own words. The way to peace must have its beginning from Jesus through His Church and her members, not simply from one human person initiating the act of consecration. Our Lady confirmed this, as already mentioned, by saying, "If my requests are heeded, Russia will be converted, and there will be peace..." Here she speaks of the two special requests; the first being the consecration *and* the second being the *First Saturdays*. It is unfortunate, to say the least, that many fail to appreciate the paramount importance of the second special request, which we are *all* called to fulfill. Fulfilling the *First Saturdays* devotion will bring about the sanctification necessary to bring true peace. Without this sanctification, a true peace is impossible.

It should be added that not far from Fatima there lived a woman named Alexandrina confined to her bed, who lived and spread the Fatima message, and especially the *First Saturdays* devotion. Through locutions in the 1930s to one who is now Blessed Alexandrina, Our Lord made known that He wanted the entire world consecrated to the Immaculate Heart of Mary. This made sense since the ideas of Communism were being rapidly spread by Russia throughout the world. Thus, the consecration of the world collegially to the Immaculate Heart of Mary with the intention of including Russia was able to fulfill Our Lady's request. St. John Paul II had this intention when he fulfilled Our Lady's request.

The fulfillment of the request for the consecration was affirmed by both Sr. Lucia in 1989 and the Church again in 2000 (*Message of Fatima*, www.vatican.va). However, there is an opinion that contests the Church's official position about the consecration. It is claimed that the consecration has not been made and that the Pope still needs to fulfill Our Lady's request.

Some also claim that St. John Paul II did not mention Russia in the consecration. It is important to note that Our Lady simply said she would ask for the consecration of Russia. However, she never said that Russia must be explicitly mentioned. Nor did she exclude an implicit consecration of Russia. Therefore, the correct interpretation would need to be left to the authority of the Church, as Sr. Lucia herself always claimed. Prior to 1984, she always objected that the consecration had not been done properly. However, she did not object to the consecration made by St. John Paul II and the bishops in 1984.

Let us now consider the consecration from another perspective. If Russia had not been consecrated in 1984, does that mean that the other nations of the world were not consecrated? Also, when the Pope included those nations in his consecration prayer "that particularly need to be thus entrusted and consecrated" (*Message of Fatima*, vatican.va), does that mean that none of those nations were consecrated? It is important to note that no nation was mentioned by name. If Russia and the other nations of the world were not consecrated, why then make a consecration at all? Of course, this wouldn't make sense.

So, if the consecration was fulfilled as the Church proclaims, it would mean that only the *First Saturdays* remains to be fulfilled. So, fulfilling the *First Saturdays* should be the focus for all of us.

We know that it is acceptable to practice the *First Saturdays* individually. Yet, if the *First Saturdays* devotion is practiced only individually, how will we know that Our Lady's request is being fulfilled? How will the world be able to credit her with the triumph? The *Communal First Saturdays* offers a solution to this problem by offering the *First Saturdays* in a communal form which bears visible witness to the practice of the *First Saturdays* while making it easier for each person and for a larger number of people to fulfill the *First Saturdays* in the way Our Lady requested. It is all too easy to forget some of the conditions when attempting to fulfill Our Lady's request. The *Communal First Saturdays* serves to help prevent such omissions.

Let us return to Sr. Lucia's words above. Our Lady continued by saying that if her requests were not fulfilled, Russia would spread her errors throughout the world. Here Our Lady gives the very reason for a special consecration of Russia at the time. Yet, as mentioned above, by the 1930s, Russia had already been spreading her errors throughout the world with a great success beyond what one might imagine (cf. Pope Pius XI, *Divini Redemptoris,* n. 17), even infiltrating the Catholic Church. With the fall of Communism in Russia in 1991, the reason for consecrating Russia in a special way no longer existed. However, many other nations continued to spread the errors of Communism throughout the world. Hence, they were in need of consecration.

It is interesting to note that in 1920, Russia (which became controlling member of the Soviet Union) became the first nation to legalize abortion since the reign of paganism. Lenin had been preaching that a woman has a right to her own body. (Of course, a baby has a distinct body of his or her own). Also, abortion became the very cornerstone of the Communist state. This legalization of abortion established the claim that rights come from the state, not God, whose very existence is denied by the Communist state.

Also, the legalization of abortion did even more than destroy the right to life, upon which all other rights are founded. The legalization of abortion became the chief means of destroying the family and denying the father's rights, since only the mother could claim "the right" to kill the child, as decided by the government. Hence, the father was denied the right to protect his child. This denial of the father's rights weakened the father's interest in taking responsibility for the family. Losing a sense of responsibility, men became more disposed to exploit women. As a result, marriage and the family became greatly weakened. In all of these ways, the Soviet government and other Communist governments gained greater control over the people by not only pretending to take the place of God but also of the family. This continues to be true in other countries today.

At the same time, the Soviet Union undermined motherhood not only by abortion but also by pressuring women to enter the labor force. With both parents missing from the home, the government had the opportunity to usurp their right to educate their own children. Also, by greatly increasing the labor pool, it was possible to pay less for labor than what the people's labor was worth. This enlarged workforce gave the appearance of government support for women, while in fact, it was enslaving them. Yet, there is a Lady, our Blessed Mother, who will give women their day and thus the rest of mankind.

Further, the government also denied the right to all forms of private property that could be accumulated by the people's labor. Heavy taxation is demanded in the *Communist Manifesto* as a means of confiscating property and centralizing power.

In addition, one of the marks of Communism is that it continuously refines its methods of deception as time and circumstances change. Control of the media and education allows Communism to shape the minds of citizens, especially the young. Communism uses many alternative names as part of the deception. It also gradually changes the meaning of the words by which it spreads its errors throughout the world.

Among those rights discussed above, as well as others denied by international atheistic Communism, there is one denial of rights, which is the most damaging of all. This denied right is the right to religious freedom, or more precisely, the right denied is to be free from coercion in the practice of religion. The denial of this most excellent right became the basis for the Communist state to persecute religion, especially the Catholic Church. This persecution places souls in jeopardy of being eternally lost because they may be deprived of the sacraments. Also, in the denial of this right, the Communist state was and is able to attempt to control or remove the greatest obstacle to the subjection of the people of the entire world to itself. This obstacle to Communism is the Catholic Church. In the Communist state's attempt to remove this obstacle, which is the Catholic Church, it has infiltrated her in an effort to gain control over her and silence her.

However, in any case, Jesus promised that "the gates of hell shall not prevail against" His Church (Mt. 16:18, *Douay Rheims*). International Communism will fail. Our Lady has promised that her Immaculate Heart will triumph and that we need the *First Saturdays* devotion for that to happen. The Fatima message is there to keep us on the narrow path.

In addition, the Catholic Church can provide a prophetic voice, which confronts governments with the standards of true justice. As a comparison, one can think of how John the Baptist confronted King Herod in defense of the family. The Church must speak the truth, even if that means martyrdom and the shedding of one's blood.

It is another Communist belief and falsehood that we progress toward a new world order by conflict. Communism claims that it is through conflict we evolve into a more perfect society. Hence, the Communists pit one group against another, one class against another, one race against another, one religion against another, non-believers against Christians, one nation against another, and even one gender or "genders" against another or "others" etc. Yet, the destruction of the family greatly accelerated with the legalization of divorce following the deterioration of Christian culture. The attack on the family is all too familiar and happening before our very eyes. Nonetheless, the Lord in His Divine Mercy wishes to bring healing to all those who have suffered so much from these attacks.

Our Lady said Russia would spread her errors throughout the world promoting wars and the persecution of the Church. Promoting wars would certainly be one major manifestation of the Communist philosophy of conflict. War can be used as a means of bringing a nation under subjection and control. Even before Russia would spread her errors, World War I so weakened Russia that it was easier for the Communist revolution to succeed in 1917. What are we to say about World War II? At the expense of her own people's lives, Russia was the real winner. World War II enabled Russia to gain control of Eastern Europe. Not long after the war, China became a Communist nation. Its own errors came from Russia. Much could be said about the other wars of the 20th century. Further, the persecution of the Church was well known in Eastern Europe, China, and in many other countries in the world. It is by far the worst persecution of the Church in history.

Today, what Our Lady warned has come to realization. The many Communist errors in the world have led to the exclusion of God in many places and the breakdown of true religion. We see the many ways that the family is attacked and destroyed. We see how the world is submerged in a flood of countless lies and deceits.

Going back to Sr. Lucia's words, Our Lady said, "The good will be martyred, the Holy Father will have much to suffer, various nations will be annihilated. In the end, my Immaculate Heart will triumph." This sentence is further developed in the third part of the secret. The next sentence concerns the promised triumph of the Immaculate Heart of Mary. Our Lady said that "in the end my Immaculate Heart will triumph." It would not be fitting for "end" to refer to the end of the world and the second coming of Jesus. The end of the world will turn our attention to the final triumph of Christ and His coming visibly in the flesh. On the other hand, Our Lady's triumph "in the end" refers to the end of the persecution of the Church and the beginning of a period of world peace, which will precede the final events in history.

It is fitting that during some period of history, there will be a triumph of grace over sin universally to show that Christ wishes to defeat Satan through the Woman. As Genesis says, "I will put enmity between you and the woman" (3:15). Also, as St. John Paul II said, "Christ will conquer through [Mary], because He wants the Church's victories now and, in the future, to be linked to her" (*Crossing the Threshold of Hope,* 1995). After Our Lady's victory, Satan and his angels will be held bound and will not be able to tempt humans such as with power and wealth. However, humans will continue to have the weaknesses of original sin and the temptations of the world, but they will be able to triumph over their sins with the help of the graces of the Holy Spirit. The faithful will triumph over sin because Our Lady will obtain these graces for them.

Our Lady continued, "The Holy Father will consecrate Russia to me and she will be converted, and a period of peace will be granted to the world." Someone might take this to mean that the consecration of Russia will bring about the period of peace. Yet, Our Lady is simply saying two things about Russia, that it will be consecrated, and that it will be converted. Our Lady did not say that the consecration alone will bring about the conversion of Russia. However, we have already seen the first stage of that conversion. It is imperative that we attend carefully to her exact words. Our Lady said, as we have seen above, "I shall come to ask for the consecration of Russia to my Immaculate Heart, and the Communion of Reparation on the First Saturdays. If my requests are heeded, Russia will be converted..." Again, Our Lady said *requests*, not request. The conversion of Russia will result from the fulfillment of the two special requests.

The *First Saturdays* devotion provides a model for the greatest way to make reparation to the Immaculate Heart of Mary. Through her Heart, we can obtain the graces of sanctification from the Lamb of God. Peace, the conversion of nations, and the salvation of souls can only result from the sanctification of the people, beginning with the Catholic Church. This is why Our Lord and His Mother have given us the *First Saturdays*. Russia's complete conversion depends upon the necessary sanctification of the Catholic Church.

The Holy Father did his part with the bishops by making the consecration. It remains for the faithful to do their part by making the

First Saturdays. At this time, it seems that a very small number are fulfilling this second special request for the *First Saturdays* and that many more will be needed to fulfill the *First Saturdays* to bring about the triumph of the Immaculate Heart of Mary. From the practice of the *First Saturdays* should arise that daily practice of the Faith that is necessary to bring peace to the world.

On any First Saturday, the faithful can fulfill this second special request individually. Yet, as the Pope and the bishops acted communally in fulfilling Our Lady's request, so it is possible for the faithful to more efficaciously fulfill the second request, the *First Saturdays*, in a communal form as well. The *Communal First Saturdays* offers an easy way to fulfill all of the conditions requested to make reparation to the Immaculate Heart of Mary. The *Communal First Saturdays* will make it easier for each person and for a larger number of people to fulfill Our Lady's request. At the same time, it will make it possible to bear witness visibly that Our Lady's request has been fulfilled when the conversion of Russia and the world takes place. In addition, as already mentioned, the communal form of the devotion will bear visible witness that the triumph has been achieved through the Immaculate Heart of Mary.

The conversion of Russia implies the reunion of the Russian Orthodox Church with the Catholic Church. The Russian Orthodox Church represents the largest segment of Byzantine churches. Its reunion with the Catholic Church should greatly influence the Greek Orthodox churches and the others as well. We cannot exclude here that these latter churches will also be encouraged to reunite with the Catholic Church more directly and by other means. In any case, not only will heeding Our Lady's requests lead to the conversion of Russia, but this heeding will also lead, as St. John Paul II said, to the Church breathing with both of her lungs. The reunion of the East and West should greatly strengthen the Church to be able to have a powerful effect upon the world and so bring peace as well as the salvation of many souls. Jesus and His Mother will spiritually reign with the saints over the world.

On the other hand, those who believe that humanity can attain the perfection of happiness within history fall into the error of millenarianism, especially in its political form. The promised peace is only for a period of time and the world still will experience the effects of original sin. This means that the period of peace will come to an end and Satan will be released and foster a falling away from the Catholic Faith, before the second coming of Christ (cf. Rev. 20:7-10). The second coming of Christ marks the time when all those who are saved will fully realize the Kingdom of God in body and soul, especially by the Beatific Vision.

Lucia's Words

"In Portugal, the dogma of the Faith will always be preserved; etc ... *[see third part of Secret below]* Do not tell this to anybody. Francisco, yes, you may tell him."

"When you pray the Rosary, say after each mystery: O my Jesus, forgive us, save us from the fire of hell. Lead all souls to Heaven, especially those who are most in need."

After this, there was a moment of silence, and then I asked:

"Is there anything more that you want of me?"

"No, I do not want anything more of you today."

Then, as before Our Lady began to ascend towards the east, until she finally disappeared in the immense distance of the firmament (brackets and italics are ours).

Commentary

The preservation of the dogma of the Faith in Portugal does not mean that Portugal itself will always be a practicing Christian country. History has proven otherwise to a certain extent. The preservation of the Faith in Portugal implies that the presence of the Shrine of Our Lady of Fatima in Portugal provides a strong reminder of the message brought from Heaven by Our Lady, influencing the teaching of faithful clergy in Portugal and elsewhere. The faithful who live the Fatima message will themselves strengthen the clergy in their Faith, before, during, and after the period of peace. The message of Fatima can be a kind of easy shortcut to the faithful adherence to Catholic dogma and practice, as found in the Deposit of Faith, and as that Deposit is interpreted by the Magisterium of the Church. With the approval of the Magisterium of the Church that it has received, Fatima is able to be a correct interpretation of many fundamental truths.

Thus, this message of Fatima can be a great help in the preservation of the Catholic Faith for people throughout the world. The *First Saturdays* plays an important role in this, especially if celebrated in the communal form. It could be too that Our Lady's words imply that Catholic dogma will not be preserved in many other places in the world, especially during the Church's trial preceding the period of peace. Since Our Lady said that the dogma of the Faith would always be preserved in Portugal, the same would apply to the period following the period of peace until the second coming of Christ.

In regard to the prayer Our Lady asked to be said after each decade of the Rosary, it is an important reminder of the reality of hell shown to the children. It is also a prayer through which we can exercise great mercy toward our neighbors by pleading that they be saved from such a terrible outcome. Most of the things we do for our neighbor are of a passing and transitory nature, but salvation is forever. What a blessing then we have in this additional prayer.

Lucia's Words

The Third Part of the Fatima Secret:

After the two parts which I have already explained, at the left of Our Lady and a little above, we saw an Angel with a flaming sword in his left hand; flashing, it gave out flames that looked as though they would set the world on fire; but they died out in contact with the splendour that Our Lady radiated towards him from her right hand: pointing to the earth with his right hand, the Angel cried out in a loud voice: 'Penance, Penance, Penance!'. And we saw in an immense light that is God: 'something similar to how people appear in a mirror when they pass in front of it' a Bishop dressed in White 'we had the impression that it was the Holy Father'. Other Bishops, Priests, men and women Religious going up a steep mountain, at the top of which there was a big Cross of rough-hewn trunks as of a cork-tree with the bark; before reaching there the Holy Father passed through a big city half in ruins and half trembling with halting step, afflicted with pain and sorrow, he prayed for the souls of the corpses he met on his way; having reached the top of the mountain, on his knees at the foot of the big Cross he was killed by a group of soldiers who fired bullets and arrows at him, and in the same way there died one after another the other Bishops, Priests, men and women Religious, and various lay people of different ranks and positions. Beneath the two arms of the Cross there were two Angels each with a crystal aspersorium in his hand, in which they gathered up the blood of the Martyrs and with it sprinkled the souls that were making their way to God (*Vatican.va*).

Commentary

Our Lady held her Heart in her right hand and the Rosary in her left. This was what Lucia told Cardinal Bertone in a second interview (*The Last Secret of Fatima*, p. 56). Again, we see from an earlier apparition that the Heart in her right hand symbolizes that Our Lady is asking for reparation to her Immaculate Heart.

Sr. Lucia's second interview with Cardinal Bertone is clearly a very important one. This interview together with the third part of the secret supplies much to ponder. In this part of the secret, we read that the splendor radiating from Our Lady's right hand puts out the fire issuing from the angel's sword. In the interview, Sr. Lucia told Cardinal Bertone, "During the vision, Our Lady was radiating light, and she held a heart in her right hand and a rosary in her left" (*The Last Secret of Fatima*, p. 56). When we combine these words with the third part of the secret above, we see that the light radiating from her right hand issued from her Heart. The light issuing from her Heart held in her right hand extinguished the flames issuing from the Angel's sword. These flames threatened to set the world on fire. This shows us that the Immaculate Heart of Mary and devotion to her Heart is protecting the world from destruction. This devotion primarily consists in the continuous practice of reparation made for the sins against the Immaculate Heart of Mary.

Let us again underline from a previous appearance that Our Lady holding her Heart is a sign of seeking reparation to her Heart. This reparation is above all realized in a Communion of Reparation on the *First Saturdays*. Reparation is also made by the other practices of the *First Saturdays,* and they help us to prepare for and intensify the reverend dispositions for Holy Communion.

The *First Saturdays* represents the highest form of reparation to the Immaculate Heart of Mary, especially if done in a communal form such as the *Communal First Saturdays*.

St. John XXIII said:

Clearly the most efficacious kind of prayer for gaining the Divine protection is prayer that is offered publicly by the whole community; for our Redeemer said: "Where two or three are gathered together for my sake, there am I in the midst of them (*Paenitentiam Agere*, n. 23).

Sr. Lucia said, "People lack peace because they lack faith, lack penance, and lack public and collective prayer" (*A Pathway Under the Gaze of Mary*, p. 247). These words may well be the result of the falling numbers of those attending religious services and other public prayer gatherings. At the same time, these words also may provide a clue in regard to the *First Saturdays* devotion and the need for a communal form, such as the *Communal First Saturdays*. Let us then make a special effort to renew public and collective prayer through the *First Saturdays* devotion in a public and communal form, in order to help obtain those graces that can help lead others back to the fulfillment of their Sunday obligation and their salvation.

Also, returning to Sr. Lucia's words, the Rosary was in Our Lady's left hand. Our Lady encourages us to pray the Rosary and to offer it in reparation to her Immaculate Heart. Our Lady has joined devotion to her Immaculate Heart and devotion of the Rosary together as an even more potent weapon against evil than the Rosary alone. This union of the two devotions is most especially practiced in the *First Saturdays* devotion.

Further, the Rosary, and especially in union with devotion to the Immaculate Heart of Mary, as part of the *First Saturdays,* is essential to Our Lady's triumph. From the devotion of the Rosary and the Immaculate Heart of Mary on the *First Saturdays*, Our Lady intends that we should obtain the grace to practice the Rosary on a daily basis. In fact, a Dominican theologian wrote an article the size of a book on the great power of combining the above two devotions together (cf. *Fatima: The Rosary and the Heart of Mary*, Marceliano Llamera, O.P., *The Thomist*, Vol. XIII, No. 4, Oct., 1950).

In the light of what was said above, the *Communal First Saturdays* provides a Rosary that gives special emphasis to the practice of devotion to the Immaculate Heart of Mary within the Mysteries. This can help the faithful become acquainted with the combination of these two devotions.

Continuing the commentary on the third part of the secret, the Angel cried out "Penance, Penance, Penance!" In the *Catechism of the Catholic Church*, we find the following explanation of penance:

> Jesus' call to conversion and penance, like that of the prophets before him, does not aim first at outward works, "sackcloth and ashes," fasting and mortification, but at the conversion of the heart, interior conversion. Without this, such penances remain sterile and false; however, interior conversion urges expression in visible signs, gestures and works of penance (n. 1430).

> Interior repentance is a radical reorientation of our whole life, a return, a conversion to God with all our heart, an end of sin, a turning away from evil, with repugnance toward the evil actions we have committed. At the same time it entails the desire and resolution to change one's life, with hope in God's mercy and trust in the help of his grace. This conversion of heart is

accompanied by a salutary pain and sadness which the Fathers called *animi cruciatus* (affliction of spirit) and *compunctio cordis* (repentance of heart) (n. 1431).

St. Thomas Aquinas shows us that penance is a virtue and the act of a virtue. This virtue and act are in the will (*S.T.*, III, q. 85, a. 1-4). Penance is thus in the will and an interior act. Penance is not an emotion of sorrow but a sorrow of the will for sin. Nonetheless, metaphorically we speak of penance as a conversion of the heart. Here, heart is taken to be a symbol of the interior life. By reflection we can discern the differences between emotion and will within ourselves. The *Catechism of the Catholic Church* continues:

> The human heart is heavy and hardened. God must give man a new heart. Conversion is first of all a work of the grace of God who makes our hearts return to him: "Restore us to thyself, O LORD, that we may be restored!" God gives us the strength to begin anew. It is in discovering the greatness of God's love that our heart is shaken by the horror and weight of sin and begins to fear offending God by sin and being separated from him. The human heart is converted by looking upon him whom our sins have pierced (n. 1432).

> "Let us fix our eyes on Christ's blood and understand how precious it is to his Father, for, poured out for our salvation it has brought to the whole world the grace of repentance" (St. Clement of Rome, *CCC*, n. 1432).

We cannot forget that penance is not our work but a work of God's grace. God in His mercy grants this grace to us, thanks to the Sacred Heart of Jesus through the mediation of the Immaculate Heart of Mary. By the grace of God, we will continue to give thanks to Him and never stop giving Him thanks.

There are many words which can be used in place of the word reparation. Penance and satisfaction are but two of them. Reparation is also a part of penance in a more complete explanation of penance (as above from *CCC* beginning with n. 1430). We see this in the following passage from the *Catechism of the Catholic Church*:

> Many sins wrong our neighbor. One must do what is possible in order to repair the harm (e.g., return stolen goods, restore the reputation of someone slandered, pay compensation for injuries). Simple justice requires as much. But sin also injures and weakens the sinner himself, as well as his relationships with God and neighbor. Absolution takes away sin, but it does not remedy all the disorders sin has caused. Raised up from sin, the sinner must still recover his full spiritual health by doing something more to make amends for the sin: he must "make satisfaction for" or "expiate" his sins. This satisfaction is also called "penance" (n. 1459).

> 'The satisfaction that we make for our sins, however, is not so much ours as though it were not done through Jesus Christ. We who can do nothing ourselves, as if just by ourselves, [we] can do all things with the cooperation of "him who strengthens" us. Thus man has nothing of which to boast, but all our boasting is in Christ . . . in whom we make satisfaction by bringing forth "fruits that befit repentance." These fruits have their efficacy from him, by him they are offered to the Father, and through him they are accepted by the Father (*CCC*, n. 1460, Council of Trent' (1551): *DS* 1691, brackets ours).

The Bishop Dressed in White

The third part of the secret also concerns the Holy Father journeying through a ruined city and up a hill to the foot of a cross where he is mortally wounded.

> John Paul II... asked for the envelope containing the third part of the secret following the assassination attempt on 13 May 1981... As regards the passage about the Bishop dressed in white, that is, the Holy Father- as the children immediately realized during the "vision"- who is struck dead and falls to the ground,

Sister Lucia was in full agreement with the Pope's claim that "it was a mother's hand that guided the bullet's path and in his throes the Pope halted at the threshold of death" (Pope John Paul II, *Meditation from the Policlinico Gemelli to the Italian Bishops*, 13 May 1994) (*Message of Fatima*, Vatican.va).

A prophecy doesn't necessarily have to come true as it seems to be predicted. God can intervene. Thus, St. John Paul II could be the Pope, as he concluded, referred to in the vision, even though he didn't die from the attempted assassination. It should also be said that a vision may sometimes not completely represent what actually happens. Ordinarily, we say that a death can only be confirmed by a doctor. It is not enough to simply look at the body. The vision was still open as to whether the person that was seen was dead or not. Thus, the Holy Father could appear to be dead in the vision but not really be dead. In some cases, we even speak of people who died and came back to life. In some of these cases also, it could be said that these persons were not really dead. In any case, it could be said that the vision was left open as to whether the Holy Father died or not. This means that the Holy Father could say that the Pope in the vision was him.

Also, in the vision, there are many bishops, priests, religious, and lay faithful who follow the Holy Father to suffer martyrdom at the foot of the Cross. Apart from the millions of unborn children who have suffered death in the past 100 years, there have been millions of martyrs in that time as well. Even now large numbers continue to be martyred. It was estimated that 90,000 died as martyrs in a recent year (2016). A kind of genocide has been taking place in the Middle East where Christianity has existed for 2000 years. Yet, as the blood of Martyrs is shed, the number of saints and their prayers grow larger in Heaven, and the Church grows stronger in its resolve to follow Christ. The Martyrs offer themselves in sacrifice to the Lord often together with whole communities of Christians and in solidarity with the Church.

On the *First Saturdays*, offering the Eucharistic Heart of Jesus to the Holy Trinity, in union with the Immaculate Heart of Mary and the Church, is a splendid way to join in solidarity with our brothers and sisters who sacrifice their lives for Christ. It can be an excellent public witness to this solidarity by practicing the *First Saturdays* in a complete communal form. The *Communal First Saturdays* is such a practice.

Proof of the Message in the Next Three Appearances and Other Occurrences

The first three visits of Our Lady provide us with the major contents of the Fatima message. The next three visits of Our Lady and other associated events emphasize the proof of the message.

The 13th of August, 1917

The children were interrogated and placed in jail, and were prevented from going to the Cova da Iria. However, even though the children were not there, a witness described what happened at the Cova da Iria that day:

> Some thought the thunder came from the road; others thought it came from the holmoak; but it seemed to me that it came from a distance. It frightened us all and many began to cry fearing they were going to be killed. Right after the thunder came a flash, and immediately, we all noticed a little cloud, very white, beautiful and bright, that came and stayed over the holmoak. It stayed a few minutes, then rose towards the heavens where it disappeared. Looking about, we noticed a strange sight that we had already seen and would see again. Everyone's face glowed rose, red, blue, all the colors of the rainbow. The trees seemed to have no branches or leaves but were all covered with flowers; every leaf was a flower. The ground was in little squares, each one a different color. Our clothes seemed to be transformed also into the colors of the rainbow. The two vigil lanterns hanging from the arch over the holy spot appeared to be of gold. When the signs disappeared, the people seemed to realize that Our Lady had come and, not finding the children, had returned to Heaven (*The*

Crusade of Fatima: The Lady More Brilliant than the Sun, De Marchi, J., 1947, p.75)

Commentary

This description of what occurred on August 13 shows us that those other than the children witnessed the thunder and flash of lightning just prior to the time when Our Lady would appear. They immediately began to see a little white cloud "which stopped for a few moments over the tree, and rose in the air until it disappeared." The little white cloud seemed to be a sign that Our Lady had come and then ascended until she disappeared. Then they saw things they had seen before and would see again. Their faces began to reflect all the colors of the rainbow and the ground also reflected various colors. The trees seemed to be covered with flowers. The lanterns fixed to the arch looked as though they had turned to gold. August 13th was not to be the only day that people witnessed such things, although October 13th was much more extraordinary.

Meanwhile, the children themselves were about to give a quite different but powerful witness to the truth of the message and the apparitions. While the children were preparing to go to the Cova, the Administrator of Ourem used deception to bring them to Ourem where they were detained for questioning. The children were threatened with death and to be executed one by one if they did not reveal the secret entrusted to them by Our Lady. As they took each child away, they would say the child was going to be fried to death. Since these men were atheists and part of an atheistic government persecuting the Church, one wonders why they would want to know the secret except that they might have thought it was a plot against the government. In any case, although the children were greatly frightened, they could not be persuaded to tell the secret even in the face of a horrible death. This is convincing proof that the children were telling the truth about the apparitions. The children of themselves could not have done what they did without powerful supernatural help.

The 15th of August, 1917

The children were released from jail on August 15th, the feast of the Assumption of Our Lady. These days of August 13-15 seem to hold a symbolic meaning corresponding to the death, resurrection, and Assumption of the Virgin Mary into Heaven. On June 25th, 1997 during a General Audience, Pope John Paul II affirmed that Mary not only experienced the assumption of her body into Heaven but also previously suffered death, stating:

> It is true that in Revelation death is presented as a punishment for sin. However, the fact that the Church proclaims Mary free from original sin by a unique divine privilege does not lead to the conclusion that she also received physical immortality. The Mother is not superior to the Son who underwent death, giving it a new meaning and changing it into a means of salvation.
>
> Involved in Christ's redemptive work and associated in his saving sacrifice, Mary was able to share in his suffering and death for the sake of humanity's Redemption. What Severus of Antioch says about Christ also applies to her: "Without a preliminary death, how could the Resurrection have taken place?" (Antijulianistica, Beirut 1931, 194f.). To share in Christ's Resurrection, Mary had first to share in his death.
>
> The New Testament provides no information on the circumstances of Mary's death. This silence leads one to suppose that it happened naturally, with no detail particularly worthy of mention. If this were not the case, how could the information about it have remained hidden from her contemporaries and not have been passed down to us in some way?
>
> As to the cause of Mary's death, the opinions that wish to exclude her from death by natural causes seem groundless. It is more important to look for the Blessed Virgin's spiritual attitude at the moment of her departure from this world. In this regard, St Francis de Sales maintains that Mary's death was due to a transport of love. He speaks of a dying "in love, from

love and through love", going so far as to say that the Mother of God died of love for her Son Jesus (*Treatise on the Love of God*, bk. 7, ch. XIII-XIV).

Whatever from the physical point of view was the organic, biological cause of the end of her bodily life, it can be said that for Mary the passage from this life to the next was the full development of grace in glory, so that no death can ever be so fittingly described as a "dormition" as hers.

There is also a common tradition among Catholics and Orthodox that Our Lady was assumed into Heaven on the third day after her death in imitation of Our Lord Who rose on the third day. We have already seen that Our Lady rose up to Heaven after each of her first three apparitions. Also, we will see that she does this again in the next three as a kind of acting out of the Assumption. As Our Lady, the Immaculate Conception, acted out each of the Mysteries of the Rosary in mime during her 15 appearances at Lourdes, so also Our Lady of the Rosary did something similar in regard to the Assumption at Fatima. Now we see a further confirmation of this as the children experienced a kind of spiritual death and resurrection during the three days of August 13-15, being set free on the feast of the Assumption. The appearances at Fatima seem to anticipate the dogma of the Assumption in 1950, while Our Lady's declaration, "I am the Immaculate Conception" at Lourdes in 1858 followed the definition of the dogma four years earlier in 1854.

The 19th of August, 1917

Lucia's Words

We were with the sheep in a place called Valinhos, when we felt something supernatural approaching and enveloping us. Suspecting that Our Lady was about to appear to us, and feeling sorry lest Jacinta might miss seeing her, we asked her brother to go and call her. As he was unwilling to go, I offered him two small coins, and off he ran.

Meanwhile, Francisco and I saw the flash of light, which we called lightning. Jacinta arrived, and a moment later, we saw Our Lady on a holmoak tree.

"What do you want of me?"

"I want you to continue going to the Cova da Iria on the 13th, and to continue praying the Rosary every day. In the last month, I will perform a miracle so that all may believe."

"What do You want done with the money that the people leave in the Cova da Iria?"

"Have two litters made. One is to be carried by you and Jacinta and two other girls dressed in white; the other one is to be carried by Francisco and three other boys. The money from the litters is for the "festa" of Our Lady of the Rosary, and what is left over will help towards the construction of a chapel that is to be built here."

"I would like to ask you to cure some sick persons."

"Yes, I will cure some of them during the year."

Then, looking very sad, Our Lady said:

"Pray, pray very much, and make sacrifices for sinners; for many souls go to hell, because there are none to sacrifice themselves and to pray for them."

And she began to ascend as usual towards the east.

Commentary

Here we see for the first time that Our Lady promises a miracle which will occur in the last month, namely, October. Now when a prophecy is made and then fulfilled before witnesses, not only the miracle, but the prophecy itself is a proof of the truth of the apparitions and the accompanying message. As always, the official approval of the Church provides for the greatest confidence that these apparitions are worthy of belief.

Lucia asked what was to be done with the money. They are to have two litters made to carry the donations. One was to be carried by Lucia and Jacinta and two others girls. The other litter was to be carried by Francisco and three other boys. The money was to be used for the feast of Our Lady of the Rosary, which is celebrated on October 7. In this way, Our Lady gives added importance to this feast, which originated from a great naval victory in 1571 over the Muslim Turks who sought to overrun Europe. Any money left over from the feast was to go toward the construction of a chapel. Such a chapel was indeed built and provided a place where Mass could be said and the Holy Eucharist could remain. This chapel was bombed in 1922 and subsequently rebuilt. The current chapel continues to display the first statue of Our Lady of the Rosary of Fatima.

Our Lady also appealed to the children's love of neighbor by asking them to pray very much and make sacrifices for sinners, for many souls go to hell because they have no one to sacrifice themselves and pray for them. Our Lady spoke of this with different words in the previous apparition but made it more explicit here. What is the ultimate value of our good deeds toward our neighbor if these acts are not offered up in our prayers and sacrifices? Our Lady will show us a special way to do this by practicing the *First Saturdays*. In turn, the *First Saturdays* will nourish the daily practice of prayer and sacrifice. Many have yet to discover the tremendous wisdom to be found in the request for and practice of the *First Saturdays*. If we are able to practice the *First Saturdays* together in a communal form such as in the *Communal First Saturdays*, we will be even more greatly blessed as discussed in the previous commentary.

The 13th of September, 1917

Lucia's Words

At last, we arrived at the Cova da Iria, and on reaching the holmoak we began to say the Rosary with the people. Shortly afterwards, we saw the flash of light, and then Our Lady appeared on the holmoak.

"Continue to pray the Rosary in order to obtain the end of the war. In October Our Lord will come, as well as Our Lady of Dolours and Our Lady of Carmel. Saint Joseph will appear with the Child Jesus to bless the world. God is pleased with your sacrifices. He does not want you to sleep with the rope on, but only to wear it during the daytime."

"I was told to ask you many things, the cure of some sick people, of a deaf-mute…"

"Yes, I will cure some, but not others. In October I will perform a miracle so that all may believe."

Then Our Lady began to rise as usual, and disappeared.

Commentary

Again, we can note that the children say the Rosary with the people in preparation for Our Lady's appearance. It would be helpful then to say the Rosary prior to Our Lord's coming in the Holy Eucharist during Mass. Again, the communal form of the *First Saturdays* would be ideal. The *Communal First Saturdays* provides such a communal form and everything necessary to get started, including books for the faithful to follow along.

As in every appearance at Fatima, Our Lady continued to ask the children to say the Rosary. It would seem that the best way to promote the Rosary is to promote the *Communal First Saturdays* since this devotion includes the public recitation of the Rosary before Mass and keeping Our Lady company during the 15-minute separate and additional meditation on the Mysteries of the Rosary after Mass. This helps a person to say the Rosary with the beads more fruitfully at other times. Further, in the *Communal First Saturdays*, the meditation on the Mysteries of the Rosary after Mass makes use of the *lectio divina* with Scripture, a practice highly recommended by the Church (cf. *CCC,* 1177, 2708, also cf. *Verbum Domini*). This helps us to call to mind Scripture when we are saying the Rosary with the beads. The use of Scripture with the Rosary is recommended by St. John Paul II.

Further, the *Communal First Saturdays* is able to promote the Rosary since the public recitation of the Rosary in the parish gives a visible witness and reminder to the faithful to say the Rosary. Also, the *Communal First Saturdays* shows the relationship of devotion to the Liturgy. Devotions, and in particular the Rosary, should lead us to the Liturgy and also be an excellent way to follow the Liturgy. As St. Paul VI said, "meditation on the mysteries of the Rosary... can be an excellent preparation for the celebration of those same mysteries in the liturgical action and can also become a continuing echo thereof" (*Marialis Cultus*, n. 48)

In conclusion, the *Communal First Saturdays* helps to promote the Rosary in the above four ways: 1) it has the communal Rosary with the beads as a way to prepare for the Liturgy, 2) it has the separate and additional communal meditation on the Mysteries of the Rosary in Our Lady's company after the faithful receive Jesus, 3) it uses the Sacred Scripture for the meditation in the form of *lectio divina*, and 4) it gives visible witness to the importance of the Rosary to the entire parish.

Moreover, the September apparition of Our Lady included prophecies that could be fulfilled in the following month. Our Lady prophesied exactly who would come in the vision of October: Our Lord, Our Lady of Dolours (Sorrows), Our Lady of Mt. Carmel, and St. Joseph with the Child Jesus to bless the world. These prophecies were fulfilled in October and thus are proofs for the message of Fatima.

However, these visions were reserved for the children to witness. The proof was manifested when the children gave identical testimony when individually interviewed. In addition, Our Lady also foretold a miracle that all might believe. In October, the miracle of the sun was witnessed by 70,000 people. Our Lady fulfilling in October before so many witnesses a prophecy she made in both August and September was itself a separate proof of the apparitions and message of Fatima.

Besides the miracle itself, one could also say that the effect of the miracle on people's lives was a kind of proof. Those who came to mock, found themselves on their knees. A great change took place in Portugal. Even a prominent atheist was converted to the

Catholic Faith and rose to the office of President of Portugal on the feast of Our Lady of Guadalupe only two months after the miracle of the sun. Sadly, he was assassinated the next year. Later, in 1926, a President was appointed who again made peace with the Church and restored traditional values.

Finally, the children had found a very rough rope which they divided up three ways so that each one could wear it around their waste as a penance. It is to this rope that Our Lady refers after saying that God is pleased with their sacrifices. Our Lady tells them not to wear the rope at night but only during the day. Possibly the rope would interfere with their sleep or even something more serious.

For centuries, there has been a practice of wearing cords around the waist. One such cord is worn by members of the Confraternity of the Angelic Warfare. This cord has a knot for each mystery of the Rosary. Thus, this cord honors Our Lady of the Rosary who gave us the message of Fatima. The cord is worn to obtain the virtue of chastity and love Truth. This confraternity originated from the story of St. Thomas Aquinas fighting off temptation against chastity and being clothed by angels with a cord. In wearing a cord, we then have three visible signs of the practices of the Fatima message. The rosary beads represent prayer, the cord represents sacrifice, and the Brown Scapular of Our Lady of Mt. Carmel represents devotion to the Immaculate Heart of Mary (cf. October 13).

The 13th of October, 1917

Lucia's Words

A little later, we saw the flash of light, and then Our Lady appeared on the holmoak.

"What do you want of me?"

"I want to tell you that a chapel is to be built here in my honour. I am the Lady of the Rosary. Continue always to pray the Rosary every day. The war is going to end, and the soldiers will soon return to their homes."

"I have many things to ask you: the cure of some sick persons, the conversion of sinners, and other things..."

"Some yes, but not others. They must amend their lives and ask forgiveness for their sins."

Looking very sad, Our Lady said:

"Do not offend the Lord our God any more, because He is already so much offended."

Then, opening her hands, she made them reflect on the sun, and as she ascended, the reflection of her own light continued to be projected on the sun itself.

Commentary

Our Lady requested that a chapel be built in her honor. A chapel is a place where the Holy Eucharist is present in a tabernacle and where Mass can be said. Here pilgrims can come not only to honor Our Lady but also to primarily worship her Son. Our Blessed Mother told us that she is the Lady of the Rosary. Again, without fail, Our Lady asks that the Rosary be said every day. The Rosary is the common thread that runs through every apparition. Reparation is mentioned in five of the six apparitions and implied in the other one. Consecration is only mentioned in one of the six appearances and implied in the October apparition, as we shall soon see. That Our Lady mentioned reparation so often and consecration only once shows a much greater emphasis on reparation. Of the two special requests, the request for the *First Saturdays* in reparation to the Immaculate Heart of Mary will receive greater emphasis than the request for the consecration of Russia, as we shall soon see.

Cures may occur in some cases but not in others. But it is necessary that all amend their lives and seek forgiveness for their sins. Then Our Lady looked very sad.

Yet, Our Lady is in Heaven and is in the state of perfect happiness. Our Lady sees God directly with her intellect, and her will rests in God with love. How then can she be sad? Yet, Our Lady is also able to apprehend the sinful state of the world. Our Lady cannot be indifferent to evil. As she loves the perfect good, she also hates what is contrary to that good. Even her emotions which are in perfect harmony with her intellect and will are repulsed by sin. The Virgin Mary's outer appearance as Our Lady of Sorrows reflects this aversion to sin. Yet, this does not compromise her perfect happiness in God. In a sense, she would not be happy if she were not repulsed by sin. Our Lady is happy that what offends God offends her. As a loving Mother, she sees the good in every person and the potential good as well. Yet, she also hates sins, which are harmful to us as a spiritual disease. Finally, Our Lady sees the good she loves and the evil she rejects within the plan of Divine Providence, and that everything is working toward the ultimate victory of God over evil (cf. Cardinal Ciappi O.P., *A Heart for All*, 1972, p. 91).

Lucia's Words

Here, Your Excellency, is the reason why I cried out to the people to look at the sun. My aim was not to call their attention to the sun, because I was not even aware of their presence. I was moved to do so under the guidance of an interior impulse.

After Our Lady had disappeared into the immense distance of the firmament, we beheld St. Joseph with the Child Jesus and Our Lady robed in white with a blue mantle, beside the sun. St. Joseph and the Child Jesus appeared to bless the world, for they traced the Sign of the Cross with their hands. When, a little later, this apparition disappeared, I saw Our Lord and Our Lady; it seemed to me that it was Our Lady of Dolours. Our Lord appeared to bless the world in the same manner as St. Joseph had done. This apparition also vanished, and I saw Our Lady once more, this time resembling Our Lady of Carmel.

Commentary

After Lucia was inspired to cry out to the people to look at the sun, the children began to see the three visions, one after the other beside the sun. These three visions can be understood to represent the

Joyful, Sorrowful and Glorious Mysteries of the Rosary, but also seem to have additional meanings.

The Joyful Mysteries are represented by the appearance of St. Joseph and the Child Jesus blessing the world by tracing the sign of the Cross with their hands. Our Lady stands beside the sun robed in white with a blue mantle. This vision and the ones that followed fulfilled what Our Lady promised in the previous month. This vision draws attention to St. Joseph and the Child Jesus blessing the world together. This symbolizes that St. Joseph also participates in bringing peace to the world. With this vision, Our Lady calls for devotion to St. Joseph. As these visions call to mind the Rosary, we see that devotion to St. Joseph can be practiced while meditating on the Rosary. As the Rosary is also a practice of the *First Saturdays*, we could say that this devotion to St. Joseph in the Rosary plays an essential part in bringing about world peace through the *First Saturdays*. For this reason, the *Communal First Saturdays* has a special prayer to St. Joseph before the recitation of the Rosary.

The Sorrowful Mysteries were represented by Our Lord blessing the world and Our Lady of Dolours (Sorrows). Here we are reminded of what Our Lady said earlier about the way God is offended by sin. In fact, Jesus was killed by our sins, and Our Lady experienced the sword of sorrow in her Heart because of our sins.

Also, the sign of the Cross in the Joyful and Sorrowful Mysteries reminds us of Emperor Constantine's vision in which he saw the sign of the Cross beside the sun and the voice that said he would conquer by this sign. On the following day in 312 A.D. a great victory was won and the Catholic Church was liberated from persecution in the Roman Empire. The visions during the miracle of the sun at Fatima seem to herald a far greater victory resulting in peace throughout the world obtained through the Immaculate Heart of Mary.

The Glorious Mysteries were then represented by the appearance of Our Lady of Mt. Carmel. Of course, Our Lady of Mt. Carmel holds the Child Jesus and is crowned as Queen. She holds out her Brown Scapular. St. John Paul II said that the Brown Scapular may be worn as a sign of consecration to the Immaculate Heart of Mary (cf. *Message of John Paul II to the Carmelite Family*, 25

March 2001). The fact that the Brown Scapular is included in a representation of the Mysteries of the Rosary could be the reason why Sr. Lucia said the Rosary and the Brown Scapular are inseparable in the Fatima message. Finally, the three visions beside the sun imply a victory of the Immaculate Heart of Mary, which includes St. Joseph and the restoration of the family, reparation to Our Lady of Sorrows, and consecration represented by Our Lady of Mt. Carmel.

Regardless of the powerful witness given by the children during their time in prison, the miracle of the sun before 70,000 people was the most impressive proof, especially for those who did not believe. Atheism was already being embraced by large numbers in Portugal. Already, in 1915, it was said that Lisbon, Portugal was the capital of atheism in the world. A similar fate was about to strike Moscow. For those who would like to have a better idea of what was experienced by the atheists who came to mock the apparitions and left converted, there are a number of eye witness accounts in writing which one may read concerning the miracle of the sun, including those in secular newspapers (cf., *Documents of Fatima and the Memoirs of Sister Lucia,* Martins and Fox, 2002; ewtn.com). One eye witness account is included here along with an excerpt from Fr. De Marchi's investigation of the miracle of the sun.

Eye Witness Account

I was looking at the place of the apparitions, in a serene, if cold, expectation of something happening, and with diminishing curiosity, because a long time had passed without anything to excite my attention. Then I heard a shout from thousands of voices and saw the multitude suddenly turn its back and shoulders away from the point toward which up to now it had directed its attention, and turn to look at the sky on the opposite side.

It must have been nearly two o'clock by the legal time, and about midday by the sun. The sun, a few moments before, had broken through the thick layer of clouds which hid it, and shone clearly and intensely. I veered to the magnet which seemed to be drawing all eyes, and saw it as a disc with a clean-cut rim, luminous and shining, but which did not hurt the eyes. I do not agree with the comparison which I have heard made in Fátima---that of a dull silver disc. It was a clearer, richer, brighter color, having something of the luster of a pearl. It did not in the least resemble the moon on a clear night because one saw it and felt it to be a living body. It was not spheric like the moon, nor did it have the same color, tone, or shading. It looked like a glazed wheel made of mother-of-pearl. It could not be confused, either, with the sun seen through fog (for there was no fog at the time), because it was not opaque, diffused or veiled. In Fátima it gave light and heat and appeared clear-cut with a well-defined rim.

The sky was mottled with light cirrus clouds with the blue coming through here and there, but sometimes the sun stood out in patches of clear sky. The clouds passed from west to east and did not obscure the light of the sun, giving the impression of passing behind it, though sometimes these flecks of white took on tones of pink or diaphanous blue as they passed before the sun.

It was a remarkable fact that one could fix one's eyes on this brazier of heat and light without any pain in the eyes or blinding of the retina. The phenomenon, except for two interruptions when the sun seemed to send out rays of refulgent heat which obliged us to look away, must have lasted about ten minutes.

The sun's disc did not remain immobile. This was not the sparkling of a, heavenly body, for it spun round on itself in a mad whirl. Then, suddenly, one heard a clamor, a cry of anguish breaking from all the people. The sun, whirling wildly, seemed to loosen itself from the firmament and advance threateningly upon the earth as if to crush us with its huge and fiery weight. The sensation during those moments was terrible.

During the solar phenomenon, which I have just described in detail, there were changes of color in the atmosphere. Looking at the sun, I noticed that everything around was becoming darkened. I looked first at the nearest objects and then extended my glance further afield as far as the horizon. I saw everything an amethyst color. Objects around me, the sky and the atmosphere, were of the same color. An oak tree nearby threw a shadow of this color on the ground.

Fearing that I was suffering from an affection of the retina, an improbable explanation because in that case one could not see things purple-colored, I turned away and shut my eyes, keeping my hands before them to intercept the light. With my back still turned, I opened my eyes and saw that the landscape was the same purple color as before.

The impression was not that of an eclipse, and while looking at the sun I noticed that the atmosphere had cleared. Soon after I heard a peasant who was near me shout out in tones of astonishment: "Look, that lady is all yellow!"

And in fact everything, both near and far, had changed, taking on the color of old yellow damask. People looked as if they were suffering from jaundice, and I recall a sensation of amusement at seeing them look so ugly and unattractive. My own hand was the same color. All the phenomena which I have described were observed by me in a calm and serene state of mind, and without any emotional disturbance. It is for others to interpret and explain them.

Dr. Almeida Garrett, PhD
(Coimbra University, ewtn.com)

From *The True Story of Fatima* by John De Marchi I.M.C.

As the miracle came to its end and the people arose from the muddy ground, another surprise awaited them.

A few minutes before, they had been standing in the pouring rain, soaked to the skin. Now they noticed that their clothes were perfectly dry. How kind was Our Lady to her friends who had braved rain and mud, and put on their very best clothes for her visit (X. Sixth Apparition, continued, 1947).

Let us consider one last question concerning the miracle of the sun. How does the miracle of the sun compare with other miracles in history? Certainly, without any doubt whatsoever, the Resurrection is the most important miracle in history. As St. Paul said, "If Christ has not been raised, then our preaching and your faith is in vain" (I Cor. 15:14). Without Faith, there is no salvation and eternal life. Yet, the miracle of the Resurrection was reserved for chosen witnesses, as many as 500. Strictly speaking, the Resurrection was not a public miracle.

The miracle of the sun at Fatima was a public miracle. It was widely publicized in Portugal beforehand and open to the general public, even the enemies of the Church who controlled the government and media. There were some 70,000 eye witnesses present that day at Fatima, including the atheistic press, which published the story. Like the Resurrection, the miracle of the sun had the rare distinction of being prophesied beforehand. In the case of the miracle of the sun, the miracle was prophesied to occur on a certain day and at a precise hour. For these reasons, it can be said that the miracle of the sun is the greatest *public* miracle prophesied to occur on an exact day and at a precise hour of any, in all of history. It was a great sign; the miracle shows Our Lady of Fatima to be the Great Sign (cf. Rev. 12:1).

The Three Apparitions after Fatima

The next three apparitions are an essential part of the complete Fatima message. The three apparitions are focused on the two special requests Our Lady referred to on July 13, 1917. Our Lady said she would come again to ask for the two special requests.

The First Post Fatima Apparition

Our Lady and the Child Jesus did come again on December 10, 1925 to ask for and explain the First Saturdays, the second special request.

Lucia's Words

On the 10th of December, 1925, the Most Holy Virgin Mary appeared to Lucia, with the Child Jesus by Her side, elevated on a cloud of light. Our Lady rested one hand on Lucia's shoulder, while in the other hand She held a heart surrounded with sharp thorns. At the same time the Child Jesus spoke:

"Have pity on the Heart of your Most Holy Mother. It is covered with the thorns with which ungrateful men pierce it at every moment, and there is no one to remove them with an act of reparation." (*Lucia Speaks on the Message of Fatima*, Ave Maria Institute, 1968).

Commentary

This appearance of Jesus and Mary on December 10th, 1925 was to Lucia in a Dorothean convent in a small city called Pontevedra, Spain. One can speculate as to why God would choose this place to fulfill Our Lady's promise made on July 13, 1917 to ask for the *First Saturdays*. For hundreds of years, pilgrims to Santiago de Compostela have come from Portugal through Pontevedra. Also, there is a tradition that long ago Our Lady appeared in the midst of the pilgrims along this route. In the 19th century, the Pilgrim Virgin chapel was built in Pontevedra. We can see that the idea of a Pilgrim Virgin was already a familiar one in Portugal in view of the Portuguese Camino (Way) to Santiago de Compostela. Also, in a kind of pilgrimage, Our Lady brought the continuation of her message from Fatima to Pontevedra by appearing there to Sr. Lucia.

It was not until 1946 that Pope Pius XII sent out two International Pilgrim Virgin statues from Fatima to the East and the

West. Many other national statues would later also be sent. This practice may have been inspired by the appearance of the Pilgrim Virgin on the way to Santiago de Compostela.

Again, we have just seen that the *First Saturdays* devotion and the Pilgrim Virgin devotion are connected at Pontevedra. This is called to mind by the *Communal First Saturdays* and the *Pilgrim Virgin Statue Church to Home Visitation*. The Pilgrim Virgin statue devotion may follow the Scripture meditation on the Mysteries of the Rosary. The Pilgrim Virgin goes forth from the *Communal First Saturdays* to establish the reign of the Sacred Heart of Jesus in the home and returns on the following Saturday with the family to the Eucharistic Heart of Jesus in the church.

It is interesting to note that the flagship of Christopher Columbus, the Santa Maria, was built in Pontevedra. Columbus brought on board a statue of the Blessed Virgin. Some say this was an image of Our Lady of Guadalupe. In Guadalupe, Spain there was a shrine in honor of Our Lady of Guadalupe with her original image before her appearance in Mexico. Here the King and Queen of Spain signed the document authorizing the journey of Christopher Columbus to the New World. Queen Isabella had made a retreat at the shrine which inspired her to grant the request of Columbus. Columbus himself made a retreat at this shrine of Our Lady of Guadalupe before embarking on his exploration.

Later, Our Lady would appear in Mexico City and be referred to as Our Lady of Guadalupe. No doubt some of the faithful were able to see the guiding hand of Our Lady from the very beginning of the journey to the New World to the time of her apparition.

Forty years later, a painted image of Our Lady of Guadalupe would travel back to Spain and be placed on the flagship of the Christian fleet, which would gain a great victory at Lepanto over the Muslim Turks in 1571. This saved Europe and changed history. Also, the great victory took place on October 7. This date became the feast of Our Lady of the Rosary.

As we see in the quotation above, the Virgin Mary appeared with the Child Jesus. In one hand Our Lady held her Heart as we have seen before in the apparitions of June and July, 1917, symbolizing her desire for reparation. In the apparition of 1925, the Child Jesus is the first one Who speaks by asking us in the person of Lucia to have compassion on the Heart of His Mother. Jesus loves His Mother before any other human being. Jesus loves us on account of His Mother and for ourselves. After the Humanity of Jesus, Our Lady is the first and greatest of His work of creation and fruit of His Redemption. If we do not appreciate the masterpiece of Jesus, then how can we appreciate Him? If we offend her, we offend Him. If we neglect her, we neglect Him. Our Lady is a Gift of Jesus' Sacred Heart to us. Not only must we love our Blessed Mother, but we also need to show this by mercifully removing the thorns of our sins from her Heart with acts of reparation. While we can make sacrifices for this intention every day, Our Lady wishes to show us a special way to do so that is most effective and even a model for other occasions.

Lucia's Words

Then Our Lady said to Lucia:

"My daughter, look at My Heart surrounded with the thorns with which ungrateful men pierce it at every moment by their blasphemies and ingratitude. You, at least, try to console me, and say that I promise to assist at the hour of death with all the graces necessary for salvation all those who, on the first Saturday of five consecutive months, go to Confession and receive Holy Communion, recite five decades of the Rosary and keep me company for a quarter of an hour while meditating on the mysteries of the Rosary, with the intention of making reparation to me." (*Lucia Speaks on the Message of Fatima*, Ave Maria Institute, 1968).

Commentary

Now Our Lady herself tells us to look at her Heart. Ungrateful men pierce her Heart at every moment with sins of blasphemy and ingratitude. This is taking place now. Our Lady asks us in the person of Lucia to try to console her. As our Spiritual Mother, Our Lady consoles us. In return, we can only try to console her. However, we can only hope and pray that our Mother will be pleased to accept our efforts to console her.

Our Lady then made another promise. Let us recall that Our Lady already made a promise on July 13, 1917 with the condition that we fulfill her two special requests. What did Our Lady promise? Our Lady promised the salvation of souls and a certain period of peace in the world. The second special request was for the *First Saturdays*. Our Lady did not mention a definite number of consecutive first Saturdays, since salvation and peace in the world require an ongoing effort of prayer and sacrifice. Through the ongoing practice of the *First Saturdays*, we can continue to show love for our neighbor. A publicly scheduled *First Saturdays* in a communal form would help to support the ongoing practice of this devotion. The *Communal First Saturdays* is designed to provide such a communal form.

On December 10, 1925, Our Lady made a second promise and also told us how to practice the *First Saturdays* devotion. Our Lady promises to assist at the hour of death, with all the graces necessary for salvation all those who fulfill four conditions, each with the intention of making reparation to her Immaculate Heart. To obtain the second promise mentioned here by Our Lady, we need to do this on five consecutive first Saturdays. It is hoped that the graces obtained by fulfilling five consecutive *First Saturdays* will also enable us to persevere in the ongoing practice of the *First Saturdays* for our neighbor and peace in the world.

Yet, from Our Lady's words, she is consoled not only by us doing these practices and receiving her promise but also by us telling others about this devotion and the promise. In other words, Our Lady wants us to tell others about the *First Saturdays*. Thus, we are not only to think of the salvation of our own soul and the salvation of others by practicing the *First Saturdays,* but we also need to *spread* the *First Saturdays*. So, in other words, Our Lady asks us not only to pray for others but also to evangelize others by spreading the *First Saturdays* devotion. In fact, we are not fully practicing the Fatima message unless we are spreading the *First Saturdays*. Also, the *First Saturdays* is the only devotion in the Fatima message that Our Lord and His Mother explicitly said to spread. We can achieve even more by spreading and starting the *Communal First Saturdays* in our own parish and in other parishes as well.

Again, to fulfill Our Lady's request for the *First Saturdays*, each of the 4 practices (1). **Confession**, 2). Five decades of the **Rosary**, 3). Reception of the **Communion of Reparation**, and 4). **Keeping Our Lady company while meditating** on the Mysteries of the Rosary for the additional and separate 15-minutes) should be done with the **intention of making reparation to the Immaculate Heart of Mary**.

The *First Saturdays* is offered as prayer and sacrifice. It is important to keep in mind that sacrifices are only offered to God. Sacrifices can be offered not only for the conversion of sinners but also in reparation for sin. The *First Saturdays* is Our Lord and Our Lady's special initiative to obtain the conversion of sinners and make reparation for sins which offend God first of all. Some of our sins which offend God are sins against our neighbor. Therefore, by the sacrifice we offer to God, we are able to try to make reparation to God for our sins against God, which include sins against our neighbor.

In addition to making reparation *to* God *for* our own sins, we can make reparation *for* other people's sins against God. Through prayer and sacrifice, as can be done in the *First Saturdays* devotion, we can help pay our neighbor's debts. This follows from the commandment to love God and neighbor. This reparation for the sins of our neighbor is an act of love for our neighbor, but it could also be a way of justly compensating our neighbor for our own sins against him or her. In either case, this could be like helping to pay off our neighbor's debts.

Yet, there could be times when the only possible way to make reparation *to* our neighbor is by offering reparation *to* God for our neighbor's sins. However, this doesn't excuse us from attempting to compensate our neighbor for any damage done to him or her personally or to his or her property.

Trying to repair *our* sins against God and neighbor is a matter of justice. When we simply try to make reparation for the sins of others, it is a matter of mercy and can be justice as well. This is a mercy and a justice Our Lord and Our Lady ask us to perform through the *First Saturdays*, which can help bring about the salvation of souls.

One could say that love effects mercy and mercy is most effective through reparation and the graces we can obtain for others.

There is another consideration of great importance to our spiritual life. The Sacrifice of the Mass together with the Communion of Reparation is the greatest opportunity to make reparation for sins against God and neighbor. Also, the reception of Holy Communion can be offered in reparation to the Immaculate Heart of Mary, especially on the *First Saturdays*. The other practices of the *First Saturdays* can also offer reparation to the Immaculate Heart of Mary.

In addition, Confession, the Rosary, and the meditation of the *First Saturdays* devotion help prepare and dispose us to receive the Holy Eucharist. The degree of sanctifying grace that we receive from the Holy Eucharist depends on how well disposed we are to receive Him.

Also, there is nothing to prevent us from making a Communion of Reparation on other days as well, especially on Sundays. Being better disposed for Holy Communion on the *First Saturdays* should make us better disposed when receiving Holy Communion at other times, including the fulfillment of our Sunday obligation. Remember, that we cannot fulfill the *First Saturdays* unless we fulfill our Sunday obligation.

Which neighbors have been most offended by sin? Jesus is a Divine Person with a human nature as well as a Divine nature. So, He is God but also a man. As a man, He would be our first neighbor, the one to Whom we are most indebted and Who has been most offended by sin. To address this debt of sin, Jesus asked St. Mary Alacoque that Communions of Reparation be offered for sins against His Sacred Heart on the First Fridays. These Communions of Reparation were requested again by Pope Pius XI in *Miserentissimus Redemptor*, as mentioned earlier. Still, this does not complete the ways in which we can offer our reparation to the Sacred Heart of Jesus. One of these ways includes another person. Let us now discuss the next neighbor to whom we are indebted.

Our first neighbor after Jesus is our Blessed Mother. The sins against our Blessed Mother, after Jesus, are the most serious of sins against our neighbor. This is so because she is the Mother of God.

This is the greatest dignity that a mere human creature can be given. The greater the dignity of a person, the greater would be the seriousness of the offense against him/her. This does not detract from the fact that all are of equal dignity in so far as they share a common human nature.

The Maternal Love of her Immaculate Heart, for God and us, is without equal among mere human beings. This Love was expressed in an extraordinary way in a special moment in history. In this moment, Our Lady freely consented in her Immaculate Heart to all grace and truth coming into the world in the Person of Jesus Christ, our Savior. For this reason, an early Father of the Church, St. Irenaeus, called her "the cause of our salvation." This should help us to understand the prayer of St. Jacinta. "Sweet Heart of Mary, be my salvation." Yet, the consent from Our Lady's Heart was only the beginning of her collaboration with the Redeemer as the Mother of the Whole Christ.

Further, Jesus so loved us that He gave us His Mother to be our Mother and proclaimed it at the Cross. Jesus said, "Behold your mother" (Jn. 19:27) as she shared in His suffering. After the Holy Eucharist, our Blessed Mother is the greatest gift of His Sacred Heart to us.

As Mother of God, she is the Immaculate road by which Jesus came to us, and so she is the Immaculate road by which we can go to Him, similar to the manner in which He is the Way to the Father. Hence, our reparation to the Immaculate Heart of Mary is a more complete devotion to the Sacred Heart of Jesus. Hence, as the Mother of God and our Spiritual Mother, our responsibility toward her is greater than toward any other mere human being or angel. This responsibility also means that we must make reparation for the sins against our Blessed Mother, the most neglected Mother in the world.

Since reparation to the Immaculate Heart of Mary is reparation to the Sacred Heart of Jesus, we are encouraged to offer our Communions in reparation to the Sacred Heart of Jesus when we offer our Communions in reparation for the sins against the Immaculate Heart of Mary. The Fatima prayers can help us to do this.

We can only try to make reparation for the sins against the Immaculate Heart of Mary, but our efforts of themselves can only fall short of compensating for the offenses against her Heart as our efforts do in trying to make reparation to the Sacred Heart of Jesus. Yet, God in His mercy can enable us to do with His grace what we cannot do of ourselves (cf. *CCC*, n. 1460). The practice of the *First Saturdays* requires the grace of the Holy Spirit obtained through the Immaculate Heart of Mary.

Our Lady promises, in addition, the graces of salvation for those who practice this devotion on five consecutive first Saturdays. However, let us not forget to show love and mercy to our neighbor by continuing to practice the *First Saturdays*, and if we can do so in a communal form as in the *Communal First Saturdays*, all the more effective it will be. By persevering in the practice of the *First Saturdays*, we can not only try to make reparation for our own sins but also for the sins of others. Above all, we hope to console the Immaculate Heart of Mary by making reparation to her for these same sins. In this way, we more completely offer reparation to the Sacred Heart of Jesus.

Let it be noted that the *First Saturdays* devotion is also offered to God in supplication for sinners. This means, through the *First Saturdays*, we are also interceding on behalf of sinners to obtain for them the grace of repentance as well as other graces.

The Second Post Fatima Apparition

The Child Jesus asked Lucia if she had spread the First Saturdays.

Lucia's Words

On the 15th of February, 1926, going there as usual, I found a child who seemed to me to be the same one whom I had previously met, so I questioned him:

"Did you ask our heavenly Mother for the Child Jesus?" The child turned to me and said: "And have you spread through the world what our heavenly Mother requested of you?"

With that, he was transformed into a resplendent

Child. Knowing then that it was Jesus, I said:

"My Jesus, You know very well what my confessor said to me in the letter I read to You. He told me that it was necessary for this vision to be repeated, for further happenings to prove its credibility, and he added that Mother Superior, on her own, could do nothing to propagate this devotion."

"It is true your Superior alone can do nothing, but with my grace she can do all. It is enough that your confessor gives you permission and that your Superior speak of it, for it to be believed, even without people knowing to whom it has been revealed."

Commentary

While Our Lady said on July 13, 1917 that she would come again to ask for the consecration of Russia and the *First Saturdays*, her first appearance after Fatima, with the Child Jesus, concerned only the *First Saturdays*. A short time later, the Child Jesus alone appeared to inquire about the *First Saturdays* only. It seems that Jesus is taking, with this second appearance, a bigger role in the request for the *First Saturdays* than even Our Lady. Jesus' concern for the *First Saturdays* will continue in the locutions to Sr. Lucia. We should not be too surprised to realize that this is something that God wants. Let us recall that Our Lady said on July 13, 1917, "God wishes to establish in the world devotion to my Immaculate Heart." The *First Saturdays* represents the foremost way to do this. The *Communal First Saturdays* provides a visible public witness that this is being done and more.

The second post Fatima apparition (February 15, 1926) can be divided into two parts in regard to the message given by the Child Jesus. The first part is in regard to spreading the *First Saturdays*. This is a follow-up on the previous apparition in which Our Lady made known her desire to spread the *First Saturdays*. So, Jesus, in the second apparition after Fatima on February 15, 1926, emphasized the great importance of doing so.

The second part of this message of Jesus, on February 15, 1926, concerning Confession, could be called the introduction to the third apparition in 1929., In discussing Confession (February 15, 1926), Jesus began to address the first of the four practices of the *First Saturdays* in reparation to the Immaculate Heart of Mary. The next three practices and the intention of the *First Saturdays* were treated with both words and images in the third apparition after Fatima (1929).

As to the first part of the message, Jesus asked Sr. Lucia if she had already "spread through the world" the devotion of reparation (the *First Saturdays*) that our heavenly Mother requested. Of course, Jesus knew that she had not been able to do very much, but He was making it known that He wanted the *First Saturdays* devotion spread throughout the world. Sr. Lucia was able to answer the inquiry by referring to many difficulties. In fact, it took Sr. Lucia more than another 13 years simply to have a pamphlet on the *First Saturdays* printed with the *imprimatur* of the bishop. This pamphlet, at least, constituted the first ecclesial approval of the *First Saturdays* devotion revealed to Sr. Lucia. Still, one could say that spreading the *First Saturdays* was very difficult to accomplish. Eventually, much more was able to be done by various organizations and what is now the World Apostolate of Fatima. Even so, it is difficult to see a widespread practice of the *First Saturdays* devotion, especially in the way Our Lady asked for it to be done. In fact, for many years, interest in the *First Saturdays* actually diminished; however, it is now starting to increase.

The difficulty in spreading the *First Saturdays* can be explained by the fact that God's plans are not our plans. While the *First Saturdays* is hardly practiced, we have seen the world become increasingly atheistic and enveloped in a culture of death. Even beyond World War II, the blood of the innocent has flown like a river, families have been destroyed, countless numbers have been martyred for the Faith, and large numbers have fallen away from the Church, to name a few of the tribulations. However, the stronger the opposition, the greater is the victory. The good news is that the worse that things become, the more we will appreciate the triumph of the Immaculate Heart of Mary. Will we participate in that triumph? Will we spread the *First Saturdays* devotion?

It is interesting that a Confessor said to Sr. Lucia that the Superior alone could do nothing. Jesus acknowledged that this is true. One could say that much of the effort made in the world is being made without asking God for help. This is a severe problem. Many think they can rely on themselves. Yet, even Jesus said, "the Son can do nothing of His own accord" (Jn. 5:19).

Yet, consider the rest of what Jesus said to Lucia. "It is true that your Superior alone can do nothing, but with my grace she can do all." It is also true that grace is a gift, a gift that God can pour out in abundance when He sees fit. If we are waiting for mankind to deserve this, then we will be sadly disappointed because it won't happen. God must make us worthy first by His grace. Here we see that everything depends on God's mercy. God offers mercy through the *First Saturdays* devotion. The *First Saturdays* devotion will flower in due time as will Our Lady's triumph. There are those who think they are in control, but God is in control.

Lucia's Words

She placed before Jesus the difficulty that some people had about confessing on Saturday, and asked that it might be valid to go to confession within eight days. Jesus answered:

"Yes, and it could be longer still, provided that, when they receive Me, they are in the state of grace and have the intention of making reparation to the Immaculate Heart of Mary."

She then asked:

"My Jesus, what about those who forget to make this intention?"

Jesus replied:

"They can do so at their next confession, taking advantage of the first opportunity to go to confession."

Commentary

Here, we see the second part of the message in this second post Fatima apparition. Lucia asked Jesus if the Confession for the *First Saturdays* can be done within eight days. Jesus said that it could even be longer than eight days. Yet, He doesn't give a definite day. It is possible that Jesus wished to leave any definite number of days to the Church to decide. The Church does give the number of days for Confession when seeking a plenary indulgence. This can change, but now the number of days is within 20 days before or after the fulfillment of the qualifying devotion for a plenary indulgence. It would make sense to use this number for the *First Saturdays* as well. This would easily allow a person to make a monthly Confession, and at the same time, have the opportunity of gaining a plenary indulgence every day (cf. *Manual of Indulgences*, USCCB). Oddly enough, in spite of what Jesus said, many still say to go to Confession within eight days.

Even though Confession may be more than eight days from the Communion of Reparation on the First Saturday, Jesus said that a person must still be in the state of grace when he or she receives Him. One can read more about the latter in the *Catechism of the Catholic Church* (n. 1415).

St. Paul provides a serious warning in this matter:

> Whoever, therefore, eats the bread or drinks the cup of the Lord in an unworthy manner will be guilty of profaning the body and blood of the Lord. Let a man examine himself, and so eat of the bread and drink of the cup. For any one who eats and drinks without discerning the body eats and drinks judgment upon himself. That is why many of you are weak and ill, and some have died. But if we judged ourselves truly, we should not be judged. But when we are judged by the Lord, we are chastened so that we may not be condemned along with the world (I Cor. 11:27-32).

If we are to examine ourselves, then we should also make use of the Sacrament of Penance, for which Jesus shed His Blood to help us receive Holy Communion worthily. Also, we need to discern the real presence of Jesus in His Body, Blood, Soul, and Divinity. Because many fail to respect the real presence, many are weak and ill, and some have died. This is not referring to a physical condition but to a spiritual condition of the soul. "Some have died" means that some are in the state of mortal sin and not the state of grace.

Finally, Jesus said that those who forget to make the intention of reparation to the Immaculate Heart of Mary "can do so at their next confession, taking advantage of the first opportunity to go to confession." This should remind us of the importance of making this intention when we fulfill each of the four conditions of the *First Saturdays*.

As was mentioned above, the second part of the message of this apparition is an introduction or beginning point for the third apparition that followed (1929). The other three practices of the *First Saturdays* and the intention will in some way be represented in the next apparition. Recall how St. John the Baptist prepared the people for Christ by calling them to repent. We are told that the people were even confessing their sins at the Jordan River (cf. Mt. 3:6). Later, John was able to point to Jesus and say, "Behold, the Lamb of God!" (Jn. 1:36). We should know that the Lamb of God is a metaphor for Jesus in the Holy Eucharist. Confession is emphasized as the starting point for the *First Saturdays*, because unless one is in the state of grace, the rest of the practices of the *First Saturdays* will not fulfill Our Lady's request. Also, it is fitting that Jesus elaborated on the practice of Confession on a separate day from the third apparition because it is the only practice that can be done on days other than the first Saturday, if needed. The other three practices must be ordinarily fulfilled on the same day.

The Third Post Fatima Apparition

Lucia's Words

June 13, 1929

> I had sought and obtained permission from my superiors and confessor to make a Holy Hour from eleven o'clock until midnight, every Thursday to Friday. Being alone one night, I knelt near the altar rails

in the middle of the chapel and, prostrate, I prayed the prayers of the Angel. Feeling tired, I then stood up and continued to say the prayers with my arms in the form of a cross.

Commentary

Up to this point in the Fatima message, making a Holy Hour before the Blessed Sacrament has not been specifically mentioned. Yet, we know that Francisco spent time in front of the Blessed Sacrament. Also, it seems that Lucia was inspired to do this often at her convent. So, there is good reason to include this as a practice of the Fatima message, especially since the Holy Hour mentioned above was blessed with a very important vision pertaining to the Fatima message. However, the Holy Hour is not explicitly required by the Fatima message.

The Holy Hour Sr. Lucia made was on every Thursday to Friday, from eleven to midnight. This is an ideal time since it imitates the vigil in front of the Blessed Sacrament on Holy Thursday. Also, this practice means that Sr. Lucia would have made a Holy Hour leading into every First Friday in reparation to the Sacred Heart of Jesus.

Above, Sr. Lucia told us that she said the prayers of the Angel:

My God, I believe, I adore, I hope and I love You! I ask pardon of You for those who do not believe, do not adore, do not hope and do not love You!

Most Holy Trinity, Father, Son and Holy Spirit, I adore You profoundly, and I offer You the most precious Body, Blood, Soul and Divinity of Jesus Christ, present in all the tabernacles of the world, in reparation for the outrages, sacrileges and indifference with which He Himself is offended. And, through the infinite merits of His most Sacred Heart, and the Immaculate Heart of Mary, I beg of You the conversion of poor sinners.

Clearly, Sr. Lucia was making acts of faith, adoration, hope, and love, and asking forgiveness for those who did not possess these virtues. In the second prayer, she was fittingly offering Jesus present in all the tabernacles of the world to the Most Holy Trinity in reparation for sins that have offended Him. In addition, Lucia was seeking graces from the Sacred Heart of Jesus through the Immaculate Heart of Mary for the conversion of sinners.

Lucia's Words

The only light was that of the sanctuary lamp. Suddenly the whole chapel was illumined by a supernatural light, and above the altar appeared a cross of light, reaching to the ceiling. In a brighter light on the upper part of the cross, could be seen the face of a man and his body as far as the waist, upon his breast was a dove also of light and nailed to the cross was the body of another man. A little below the waist, I could see a chalice and a large host suspended in the air, on to which drops of blood were falling from the face of Jesus Crucified and from the wound in His side.

Commentary

One could say that Sr. Lucia saw a representation of what she was already praying. The Holy Trinity is represented in the vision. On the upper part of a Cross Sr. Lucia sees a man's face and the body to the waist. This represents the Father. Sr. Lucia sees a dove of light on the man's breast, and this represents the Holy Spirit. Sr. Lucia saw another man nailed to the Cross representing the Son. Sr. Lucia also saw a large host, below the waist, upon which drops of blood fell from the face and the side of the man who represented Jesus. The large host and drops of blood represent the Holy Eucharist. The Holy Eucharist is the greatest Gift of the Sacred Heart of Jesus and this is represented by the Blood flowing from His side. The Cross of light is not mentioned in her prayer, but she does pray with her arms outstretched in the form of a cross. In this way the prayer of the Angel is able to represent the Sacrifice of Jesus and the offering of the Holy Eucharist to the Holy Trinity.

While Jesus no longer sheds His blood, He continues to offer Himself in the Mass in an unbloody way. The Holy Eucharist is not only to be offered but to be received. When the children were taught the prayer, Most Holy Trinity…, they were then given Holy

Communion and asked to make reparation for sin. The children then repeated the prayer again, in which they offered the Holy Eucharist in reparation for sin. Thus, they offered a Communion of Reparation to the Holy Trinity. This could be understood as a Communion of Reparation for the sins against the Sacred Heart of Jesus. Yet, in a similar manner, through the *First Saturdays* devotion, Our Lady taught Sr. Lucia to offer a Communion of Reparation for the sins against Her Immaculate Heart, which ultimately is in reparation to the Sacred Heart of Jesus.

Lucia's Words

These drops ran down on to the host and fell into the chalice. Beneath the right arm of the cross was Our Lady and in her hand was her Immaculate Heart. (It was Our Lady of Fatima, with her Immaculate Heart in her left hand, without sword or roses, but with a crown of thorns and flames). Under the left arm of the cross, large letters, as if of crystal clear water which ran down upon the altar, formed these words: "Grace and Mercy."

Commentary

Again, we see Our Lady with her Heart in Her hand symbolizing her appeal for reparation to Her Immaculate Heart. Sr. Lucia states that it is Our Lady of Fatima. But let us remember that Our Lady of Fatima identified herself as the Lady of the Rosary. In this sense, the vision represents the request to say the Rosary. Except for Confession, already singled out in the previous apparition, the conditions and intention of the *First Saturdays* were represented in this last vision. The Communion of Reparation can be called to mind in the prayer as well as in the vision. The additional meditation on the Mysteries of the Rosary in Our Lady's company can also be brought to mind by the Mystery of the Crucifixion and also by the Mystery of the Institution of the Holy Eucharist. Finally, the intention of making reparation to the Immaculate Heart of Mary on the *First Saturdays* and at other times is sought by Our Lady holding Her Heart in Her hand.

Finally, in the vision, under the left arm of the Cross, the flow of grace and mercy is represented. In dying for us, Jesus showed His great mercy. By dying on the Cross, Jesus merited the graces for our salvation and peace. Jesus also showed in this vision that this grace and mercy comes to us through the Sacrifice of the Mass and Holy Communion. This grace and mercy from the Holy Eucharist come to us by the intercession of the Immaculate Heart of Mary, as seen beneath the Cross in this vision. This reception of grace and mercy is especially possible when we fulfill our Sunday obligation, practice the *First Saturdays*, and any other time we attend Mass and receive the sacraments.

Lucia's Words

I understood that it was the mystery of the Most Holy Trinity which was shown to me, and I received lights about this mystery which I am not permitted to reveal.

Our Lady then said to me:

"The moment has come in which God asks the Holy Father, in union with all the Bishops of the world, to make the consecration of Russia to my Immaculate Heart, promising to save it by this means. There are so many souls whom the Justice of God condemns for sins committed against me, that I have come to ask reparation: sacrifice yourself for this intention and pray."

Commentary

Sr. Lucia understood that it was the Mystery of the Holy Trinity which was shown to her. The Holy Trinity is manifested to us by breaking into time and history through the Incarnation of Jesus Christ. Jesus' ultimate sacrifice on the Cross manifests the love between the Father and the Son, a love which is the Person of the Holy Spirit. By His crucifixion, Jesus reveals the Holy Trinity to us in the most sublime way the human mind can understand in this life.

The vision can help us understand that by offering us His Body and Blood, Jesus is also offering us the life of the Holy Trinity. For Jesus reveals from the Cross, in the vision, that where He is, there also is His Father and the Holy Spirit. Jesus said, "If a man loves me, he will keep my word, and my Father will love him, and we will come to him, and make our home with him" (Jn. 14:23). Jesus comes to us in the Holy Eucharist, the greatest Gift of His Sacred Heart, made possible by His death on the Cross. In receiving Jesus, we also receive the Father and the Holy Spirit. In receiving Jesus in the Blessed Sacrament, there can be an increase in sanctifying grace in the soul. The Holy Spirit imparts and sustains this life of grace. Where the Holy Spirit is present, there also are the Father and the Son. It is by grace that the Holy Trinity remains within us. Thus, we may speak of the indwelling of the Holy Trinity.

In the meditation after Mass, the *Communal First Saturdays* draws attention to the indwelling of the Holy Trinity that is present in a special way when Jesus is present in the Holy Eucharist within us. For where Jesus is, there is the Father and the Holy Spirit also. The presence of Jesus within us in the Holy Eucharist for an indefinite period of time after Mass makes it possible for us to continue to receive the graces imparted by Him in the Holy Sacrament.

Before discussing this apparition, we discussed two apparitions after Fatima which only concerned the *First Saturdays*. In this third apparition after Fatima, we have mentioned explicit and implicit requests concerning reparation to the Immaculate Heart of Mary and other practices related to the *First Saturdays*, at the center of which is the Holy Eucharist. After Sr. Lucia was shown what she understood to be the vision of the Holy Trinity, Our Lady then fulfilled her promise to ask for the collegial consecration of Russia to her Immaculate Heart in only one sentence. However, it is clear that the greatest emphasis has been placed upon the *First Saturdays* in this last apparition after Fatima, and solely on the *First Saturdays* in the previous two apparitions. This emphasis on the *First Saturdays* makes sense since it is through prayer and sacrifice that we can manifest our love for God and neighbor. It is through prayer and sacrifice that we not only make supplication for sinners but also offer reparation to God. The highest form of worship and reparation we can offer to God is the Sacrifice of the Mass together with the reception of Holy Communion. We can be prepared for the Lamb by Confession and the prayer of the Rosary, which we can fulfill as part of the *First*

Saturdays devotion.

On July 13, 1917, Our Lady said she would come to ask for the consecration of Russia to her Immaculate Heart and that the Holy Father would do it. On June 13, 1929, Our Lady gave the more complete explanation of this special request. Our Lady told us that the Holy Father must make the consecration of Russia to her Immaculate Heart together with the bishops of the world. This is what is called a collegial act of consecration. In a way, this anticipated an emphasis made by the Second Vatican Council on collegiality (cf. *Lumen Gentium*).

Attention should be drawn to the fact that a collegial act is also a communal act. On March 25, 1984, St. John Paul II did make the consecration in union with the bishops of the world.

While not necessary to fulfill Our Lady's special request in 1984, the priests and lay faithful were invited to join with their bishops in making the consecration and to include their own personal consecration to the Immaculate Heart of Mary. This in fact was done publicly in many places in the world. However, the participation of the faithful was not required to determine if the special request had been fulfilled.

If one has not already made their own personal consecration to the Immaculate Heart of Mary, it is still possible to join one's consecration to the collegial act. In a sense, this personal act of consecration to Jesus through the Immaculate Heart of Mary is a more explicit renewal of one's baptismal consecration to Jesus through the Immaculate Heart of Mary.

One could say that comparing a consecration in whatever form and the *First Saturdays* is in a limited way like comparing Baptism and the Holy Eucharist. Baptism includes the consecration of the one baptized. The Holy Eucharist is Jesus Himself offering a Sacrifice of Reparation on the *First Saturdays*, Sundays, and on other days. In doing so, Jesus offers us the opportunity to join His offering through the priest and to also make a Communion of Reparation. Consecration is the most necessary and reparation is the most excellent. Let us then begin with consecration and continue with reparation.

In the year 2000, the Church officially confirmed that the collegial consecration to the Immaculate Heart of Mary had been fulfilled (*Message of Fatima*, vatican.va). In addition, the Vatican wrote:

> Sister Lucia personally confirmed that this solemn and universal act of consecration corresponded to what Our Lady wished (*"Sim, està feita, tal como Nossa Senhora a pediu, desde o dia 25 de Março de 1984"*: "Yes it has been done just as Our Lady asked, on 25 March 1984": Letter of 8 November 1989). Hence any further discussion or request is without basis (*Message of Fatima*, vatican.va).

In 1989, when Sr. Lucia made this statement, Communism in the Soviet Union was already in the process of crumbling, to the astonishment of the world. The persecution of the Church there was coming to an end, as Jesus had promised Sr. Lucia (cf. below, Letter of May 29, 1930, p. 99). Jesus never told Sr. Lucia that the collegial consecration alone would bring about the *conversion* of Russia, but rather, it would end the persecution. This conversion would require the fulfillment of both special requests.

Above, Our Lady said she promises to save Russia by the consecration. We could say Russia has been saved from Communism in an incredibly marvelous way, and yet will be completely saved when we have sufficiently practiced the *First Saturdays*. Being completely saved depends on the fulfillment of both special requests, required for a period of peace and the salvation of souls. Also, Russia being completely saved means that the Russian Orthodox Church will be in full communion with the Roman Catholic Church. This union will lead to the entire nation being transformed under the reign of Christ the King. This presupposes the purification and renewal of the Catholic Church by the *First Saturdays*.

Finally, in this 1929 vision, Our Lady closed her communication by again appealing for reparation to her Immaculate Heart because so many souls are condemned by the justice of God for their sins against her. Our Lady asked that Sr. Lucia also sacrifice herself for this intention of making reparation to her, and pray. The *First Saturdays* devotion, as introduced by Our Lady, represents the ultimate form of reparation to the Immaculate Heart of Mary. Reparation to the Immaculate Heart of Mary is a more complete way of making reparation to the Sacred Heart of Jesus. The reasoning for this is the following. The Maternal Heart of Mary is a gift of the Sacred Heart of Jesus, and so He is offended when His gift is rejected. When Jesus' gift is rejected, His Sacred Heart is rejected. This requires reparation also. Thus, any reparation to the Immaculate Heart of Mary is reparation to the Sacred Heart of Jesus.

Lucia's Words

Later in an intimate communication, Our Lord complained to me, saying:

"They did not wish to heed my request!... Like the King of France, they will repent and do it, but it will be late. Russia will have already spread her errors throughout the world, provoking wars, and persecutions of the Church: the Holy Father will have much to suffer."

Commentary

The above words seem to be from a communication that took place after the 1929 vision. Our Lord predicted that the request for the consecration would not be heeded for a long time and that Russia would have already spread her errors throughout the world. This prophecy was certainly fulfilled.

As time went on in the 1930s, as mentioned earlier, Russia was already spreading her errors throughout the world so that the whole world was absorbing Communist ideas often without even realizing it. With this in mind, it would seem reasonable that the Holy Father consecrate the world to the Immaculate Heart of Mary. In 1935, Blessed Alexandrina, totally dedicated to the Fatima message, received a private revelation from Jesus that the world should be consecrated by the Holy Father to the Immaculate Heart of Mary (Pasquale, Humberto, *Beata Alexandrina*, 9th Ed., [Editor: Edições Salesianas] p. 22). Under the influence of Blessed Alexandrina's spiritual director, the bishops of Portugal wrote to Pope

Pius XI asking for the consecration of the world to the Immaculate Heart of Mary (cf. *Documents on Fatima & the Memoirs of Sr. Lucia* by Fr. Martins & Fr. Fox, 2002, p. 366). On December 2, 1940, in her letter to Pope Pius XII, Sr. Lucia asked for the consecration of the world to the Immaculate Heart of Mary with a special mention of Russia and that this be done in union with the bishops of the world (cf. *Documents on Fatima & the Memoirs of Sr. Lucia* by Fr. Martins & Fr. Fox, 2002, p. 386).

St. John Paul II preserved the intention of consecrating the world with a special mention of Russia to the Immaculate Heart of Mary when he joined with the other bishops in 1984. In the written consecration, there is special reference to those nations "that particularly need to be thus entrusted and consecrated" (*Message of Fatima*, vatican.va). The Holy Father said later that he specifically intended to consecrate Russia when he made the consecration. When Communism did fall in the Soviet Union, of which Russia was a part, much of the rest of the world continued to be severely infected with Communist ideology. However, Our Lord's promise to Sr. Lucia was more than fulfilled in Russia (cf. below, May 29, 1930, p. 99). The end of persecution in itself indicates that the consecration was fulfilled. The persecution also ended in many other countries that were in alliance with Russia.

Thus, the Pope and the bishops have done their part with good effect. Further, the Pope and the bishops carried out the first request collegially which was to do so in a communal way. Now the faithful must do their part to complete the work, including the fulfillment of the second special request, namely, the *First Saturdays*. Why not attempt to fulfill the second special request in a communal way also? The *First Saturdays* devotion needs to be visible and public. Also, Sr. Lucia affirmed that our prayer and penance need to be public and communal. The *Communal First Saturdays* makes this possible.

Letters and Locutions

Unless otherwise noted, the text from the letters and locutions below are quoted from *Documents on Fatima & the Memoirs of Sr. Lucia* by Fr. Martins & Fr. Fox, 2002. A commentary is offered for some of the selected texts.

The following are Sr. Lucia's letters which refer to the *First Saturdays*. The main emphasis in her letters during the late 20s, 30s and into the 40s is on the *First Saturdays* and the consecration of Russia and the world to the Immaculate Heart of Mary. In fact, in these letters, we see that Our Lady's two special requests first mentioned on July 13, 1917 are emphasized more than any other practice of the Fatima message. This underlines the importance of the two special requests. However, the request for the *First Saturdays* has received the greater emphasis of the two in the entire message as a whole and in her known letters up to 1945. One of these requests, the consecration, has been fulfilled. Thus, one special request remains, namely, the *First Saturdays*. If we could take a medicine that would cure the diseases of war and hatred in the world, wouldn't we take it? Such a medicine is the *First Saturdays*.

Is the *First Saturdays* a cure for the world merely because in her appearances, Our Lady proposed the *First Saturdays* as one of the two special requests that would result in the salvation of souls and a period of peace? Without any reference to Our Lady's apparitions, St. John Paul II said, "Christ will conquer through [Mary], because He wants the Church's victories now and in the future to be linked to her" (*Crossing the Threshold of Hope*, 1995). St. John Paul II also taught that Our Lady mediated all graces; so, it is only just that we should recognize the Church's victories as coming through her. Yet, would this require the *First Saturdays* devotion?

It is a revealed fact that Our Lady suffered with her Son because of our sins. St. Luke gives us a glimpse of this: "And thy own soul a sword shall pierce, that out of many hearts, thoughts may be revealed" (Lk. 2:35, *Douay Rheims*). Our thoughts about the piercing of Our Lady's Heart need to be revealed. There is an injustice against Our Lady as well as against Our Lord due to our sins. The injustice needs to be addressed in order for Our Lady to triumph and bring peace and salvation to the world. By practicing the *First Saturdays*, we attempt to make reparation in the most potent form for those sins. This is possible, first and foremost because of the Communion of Reparation. At the same time, the *First Saturdays* devotion includes other important practices which help dispose the faithful to a more fruitful reception of Holy Communion, as we have already discussed. Thus, the *First Saturdays* can be the best cure not only for individuals but also for entire nations, with the understanding that the *First Saturdays* includes the fulfillment of the Sunday obligation.

February, 1926, letter on the *First Saturdays*, an account of the *First Saturdays* apparitions.

On July 24, 1927, Sr. Lucia wrote a letter to her mother introducing her to the *First Saturdays* as well as urging her to practice the devotion and tell others about it. Lucia already thought that the separate 15-minute meditation might seem difficult to many people.

> It is the fifteen minutes to my mind, that is going to give the most confusion. But it is very simple. Who is not able to think on the Mysteries of the Rosary? On the annunciation of the angel and on the humility of our dear Mother, who, on seeing Herself so praised, called Herself a slave? On the passion of Jesus, Who suffered so much for love of us? And our Most Holy Mother near Jesus on Calvary? Who is not able then, with these holy thoughts, to spend fifteen minutes, near this most tender of mothers? (p. 277).

Commentary

The above words show us how simple the fifteen-minute meditation can be in Our Lady's company. It doesn't necessarily require any difficult methodology or deep theological questions or dialogue with Our Lady. It doesn't even require a book. At the same time, the meditation is open to a variety of different approaches which can be beneficial. The *Communal First Saturdays* includes a communal meditation after Mass. This meditation is also easy since the faithful are guided through it step by step. It also affords the faithful the opportunity to make use of Scripture which is the source of the Mysteries of the Rosary. St. John Paul II recommended using Scripture before each decade of the Rosary. The separate meditation on the Mysteries of the Rosary provides an even greater opportunity to use significantly more Scriptural texts. While the use of Scripture is highly recommended by the Church, the Church also recommends the use of the ancient *lectio divina* as a method of meditating on the

Scripture. Thus, the *Communal First Saturdays* employs the *lectio divina* in guiding the faithful through the communal meditation. The same could be done in an individual meditation.

One of the great advantages of this communal meditation on the Scripture is that it greatly helps our meditation on each decade when we say the Rosary with the beads at other times. While saying the Rosary with the beads, we can more easily call to mind the Scripture we learned in the *lectio divina*. The *lectio divina* also helps us to increase our use of Scripture, which is an important help to our spiritual growth and the work of evangelization. Thus, we can help fulfill the apostolate given to us through Baptism and Confirmation.

November 1, 1927, letter to Sr. Lucia's godmother. Sr. Lucia explained the *First Saturdays* and asked her godmother to spread it. Sr. Lucia said that she never felt so happy as when the first Saturday arrived. By the *First Saturdays*, we can try to give Jesus and Mary the consolation of being loved.

Commentary

It is important to note that Jesus and His mother gave as much emphasis or more to spreading the *First Saturdays* as to practicing the *First Saturdays*. In other words, to fulfill the Fatima message we must not only practice the *First Saturdays* but spread the *First Saturdays*. This is more important now than ever if the world is to recover from its spiritual illness. Are you spreading the *First Saturdays*? The *Communal First Saturdays* is the best way we know how to do this since it makes it easier for each person to fulfill Our Lady's request, and makes it easier for a larger number of people to do so.

December 17, 1927, on this date Sr. Lucia heard a locution from Jesus. Afterwards, Sr. Lucia wrote a letter describing this locution. In the locution, Jesus instructed Sr. Lucia to write about the *First Saturdays* while maintaining the rest of the secret of July 13, 1917 as secret. Sr. Lucia then described the first two apparitions after Fatima concerning the *First Saturdays*.

May 29, 1930, letter and locution on the *First Saturdays*. Sr. Lucia again explained the *First Saturdays* devotion in detail. Sr. Lucia understood from Jesus in the locution that after the consecration of Russia and when the persecution ceases, **"In response to the end of this persecution, His Holiness is to promise to approve of and recommend the practice of the already mentioned devotion of reparation"** (p. 281, bold is ours). Sr. Lucia mentioned Jesus' request two times in the letter. The first time Sr. Lucia mentioned it, she spoke of being urged by the Lord to ask the Holy Father to approve the *First Saturdays*. We will see later that Sr. Lucia requested Pope Pius XII to bless and extend the devotion throughout the world. However, the Lord said that the Holy Father should fulfill this request after the consecration is made and the persecution in Russia ends.

Commentary

While the faithful are asked to fulfill the *First Saturdays*, we see in the above letter and locution that the Holy Father has a role to play in approving and recommending the *First Saturdays*. Bishops have approved the *First Saturdays*. The *First Saturdays* devotion is mentioned in the text of the second part of the secret given on July 13, 1917 on the Vatican website (*Message of Fatima*, vatican.va). Also, *The Directory on Popular Piety and the Liturgy* issued under St. John Paul II may also be understood to grant approval by referring to the five *First Saturdays*.

However, at this writing, there has not been an official statement by any Pope concerning the *First Saturdays* devotion revealed in 1925. This seems remarkable when one considers that two Popes indulgenced two First Saturday devotions before a different version of the *First Saturdays* devotion was explained in 1925. However, these indulgences are no longer current since new norms were issued after the Second Vatican Council. One may now more easily gain a plenary indulgence by simply saying the Rosary under the usual conditions (cf. *Manual of Indulgences*).

Indeed, the Church's continued support for the Rosary and the considerable attention that she has given to the Fatima message are most encouraging. We look forward to the fulfillment of each step leading to peace and salvation. Nonetheless, in what remains to be done, God's ways are not our ways. We can be confident that Divine Providence is at work every step of the way for the greater glory of God.

In addition, St. John Paul II and the bishops have fulfilled the first special request for the consecration with impressive results, namely, the fall of the Soviet Union and the end of religious persecution in the Eastern Bloc. This means that persecution not only stopped in Russia but also in many other countries that were in alliance with Russia.

It is important to realize that before its collapse, the Soviet Union comprised 15 republics including Russia. In addition, there were another 7 independent nations controlled by the Soviet Union. These consisted of East Germany, Bulgaria, Poland, Hungary, Czechoslovakia, Romania, and Albania. Albania broke away in the 50s and temporarily aligned itself with Communist China. Yugoslavia developed its own independent form of Communism. All of these countries were inside the so-called "Iron Curtain" that separated Eastern and Western Europe.

The events leading to the collapse of the Soviet Union and its allies began almost immediately after the consecration on March 25th, 1984. Only weeks later, a Soviet nuclear missile site blew up in the Pacific on **May 13th**, 1984. For the Soviets, this effectively meant the end of the tense arms race, which nearly resulted in a nuclear holocaust the year before. In the following year, 1985, Gorbachev was placed in power, and he began seeking nuclear treaties. He also introduced a restructuring and free speech.

Even before the collapse of the Soviet Union, Eastern Europe found itself increasingly free (1985-1989). All of the Republics of the Soviet Union and the other seven nations were freed from Communist control and became independent democratic nations. It was of special significance that the Berlin wall, which divided East Germany from West Germany, came down in 1989. The two countries were reunited in 1990. 1989 was a key year for freedom in Poland and many other countries. The Soviet Union ended in 1991 on December 25th. Shortly before, Communists attempted a coup on August 19, 1991, the anniversary of Our Lady's appearance at Fatima, but failed on August 22, the feast of the Queenship of Our Lady.

As we can see, the result of the consecration was even greater than Jesus promised. Whatever was promised by the collegial consecration has been accomplished, and more so. This shows the infinite mercy of God in granting even more than He promises. The collapse of the Soviet Union and return of religious freedom are themselves clear proof that the collegial consecration was accomplished. At present, Russia continues to grow more Christian while much of the rest of the world succumbs to the errors of Communism.

However, the fulfillment of the second special request will bring about the *complete* conversion of Russia. Yet, there is something that must be done before the second request is fulfilled. Jesus asked in the locution cited above that when the persecution ends the Holy Father is to promise to approve and recommend the *First Saturdays*.

The *First Saturdays* seems to merit public acknowledgement by the Holy Father at least equal to that given to the collegial consecration, since the *First Saturdays* is the more important of the two special requests in the Message of Fatima. We can be confident that the result of this public attention to the *First Saturdays* will be a greater participation in the *First Saturdays* and help lead to the triumph of the Immaculate Heart of Mary.

Yet, it should also be pointed out that while there has been a rather large effort made to gather millions of petitions for the dogma of Our Lady's Spiritual Motherhood, there are no public efforts that compare with the latter for the *First Saturdays* at the time of this writing. The use of petitions to the Holy Father regarding the *First Saturdays* may be helpful. Nonetheless, Our Lord told Lucia that the approval and recommendation of the *First Saturdays* (as explained on December 10, 1925) is to be in response to the ceasing of persecutions in Russia. This persecution has stopped. Let us pray that the hour will come when the Holy Father will personally approve and recommend the *First Saturdays* as Jesus requested, so that a greater number of the faithful will participate in the devotion.

June 6, 1930, letter on the *First Saturdays*. Sr. Lucia presented questions to Jesus such as, why five *First Saturdays*? Jesus gave the following reasons for the number five:

> Daughter, the motive is simple: There are five kinds of offenses and blasphemies spoken against the Immaculate Heart of Mary.
>
> > 1st: Blasphemies against the Immaculate Conception.
> >
> > 2nd: Against Her Virginity.
> >
> > 3rd: Against the Divine Maternity, refusing, at the same time, to receive Her as the Mother of mankind.
> >
> > 4th: Those who seek publicly to implant, in the hearts of children, indifference, disrespect, and even hate for this Immaculate Mother.
> >
> > 5th: Those who revile Her directly in Her Sacred Images. Here, dear daughter, is the motive that led the Immaculate Heart of Mary to petition Me to ask for this small act of reparation. And, out of regard for her, to move My mercy to pardon those souls who have had the misfortune to offend her. As for you, seek endlessly, with your prayers and sacrifices, to move Me to mercy in regard to these poor souls (p. 284; The date of June 6th was inserted by Fr. Gonçalves).

Commentary

While these are sins directly against the Immaculate Heart of Mary, there are many other sins that follow from these sins. For example, sins against the first three, the Immaculate Conception, Virginity, and Divine Maternity can have a significant relationship to the sins of abortion and contraception.

The Immaculate Conception reminds us that Our Lady was conceived without original sin but also that she existed as a person at her conception. Hence, she had the right to life.

Our Lady's Virginity was a condition for the Incarnation and also reminds us of the importance of chastity. Such a consciousness could eliminate many abortions and also the use of contraceptives.

We should be careful to note that the third kind of offense is not only against the Divine Maternity but also against Our Lady as our Spiritual Mother. The belief that Our Lady is the Mother of God defends the dogma that Jesus is God, the foundation of all that we believe. Also, in consenting to be the Mother of God, Our Lady brought us Salvation. Further, such sins against Mary's Motherhood attacks all motherhood of which Our Lady is the exemplar. If one attacks the best mother of all, one attacks all mothers. Also, honoring Our Lady's Motherhood should strengthen one's commitment to preserving the life of the unborn child. For Our Lady's motherhood inspires an appreciation of one's own motherhood in caring for the child.

We should not forget that the third kind of offense against the Immaculate Heart of Mary includes the fact that she is the Spiritual Mother of all. What does this mean? Our Lady is our Spiritual Mother by cooperating in our Redemption, as the one who mediates all graces to us, and as our Advocate before God. Our eternal salvation depends upon this Motherhood. Yet, Our Lady is the worst treated and most neglected Mother in the world. We cannot let this continue.

Also, such sins against the Immaculate Heart of Mary can lead to a form of feminism which downgrades motherhood and virginity. These sins have a corruptive effect on our society. We now walk through the ruins of that society.

The fourth kind of offense, in regard to Our Lady's relationship with children, refers to something done publicly. One of the ways this is done is by the blasphemies against Our Lady spread through the various media. This is something that we can associate with the workings of Satan. Remember that there is enmity between the woman and the serpent (Gen. 3:15). In the book of *Revelation*, we see that Satan stands before the woman waiting to devour her child and then pursues the woman (Rev. 12:4, 13).

As Our Lord said, the motive for the five consecutive first Saturdays is to make reparation for the five kinds of offenses against

Our Lady. The fifth kind of offense is against Our Lady's Sacred Images. The *Communal First Saturdays* extends this reparation further by the Pilgrim Virgin Statue Church to Home Visitation following the 15-minute meditation. Through this devotion, Our Lady seeks to extend the reign of the Sacred Heart of her Son in the homes of the faithful. On the following Saturday, Our Lady, represented by the statue, returns to the church with the family to lead them to the Eucharistic Heart of Jesus.

Immediately after naming the fifth offense against the Immaculate Heart of Mary, Jesus said, "Here is the motive." So, it might seem as if Jesus is referring to the sins against Our Lady's Sacred Images only. However, at the very beginning, Jesus refers to "the motive" for five *First Saturdays*, namely, the five kinds of offenses against the Immaculate Heart of Mary. For these five offenses, Our Lady asked for this "small act of reparation." Practicing the five *First Saturdays* is a "small act of reparation" in that it cannot entirely compensate for the gravity of the sins against the Immaculate Heart of Mary. Nonetheless, in return for this "small act of reparation" we are each promised the graces of salvation. We are also encouraged to continue the *First Saturdays* for others. When a sufficient number of people, known to God, have practiced a sufficient number of *First Saturdays*, Our Lady promises to obtain the salvation of many souls and a certain period of peace in the world. Through the power of public prayer, the *Communal First Saturdays* hopes to add to the value of that reparation and more quickly obtain these promises.

Though we may not be able to provide a just compensation for sin, we hope that by trying to satisfy justice that we may obtain God's mercy. Above, Jesus urges us to endlessly seek, with our prayers and sacrifices, to move Him to mercy for those who have offended His Mother. This request of Jesus in the context of the motives for the *First Saturdays* would also encourage us to continue to practice the *First Saturdays* indefinitely. Keep in mind also that the Immaculate Heart of Mary has been pierced by all sins.

Lucia also asked Jesus, "And who is not able to fulfill all the conditions on a Saturday, will they not be able to do it on a Sunday?" Jesus replied, "It will be equally acceptable the practice of this devotion on the Sunday following the first Saturday, when my priests for a just reason, so grant it to souls" (*Documents of Fatima and the Memoirs of Sister Lucia,* Martins and Fox, 2002, p. 284). Not only would following Jesus' directive help prevent laxity in regard to this devotion, but it would also afford priests the opportunity to become more conscious of this devotion. This contact with the priest might also provide the opportunity to discuss the *First Saturdays* in greater detail and possibly interest the priest in supporting this devotion in some way.

October 28, 1934, letter concerns the *First Saturdays*. The Bishop of Leiria promised to promote the *First Saturdays*. Sr. Lucia forgot to talk to him about the consecration of Russia.

May 26, 1935, letter concerns the *First Saturdays*. Sr. Lucia said she wrote to the Bishop to remind him of his promise of a publication on the *First Saturdays*. Sr. Lucia was very intent upon spreading this devotion of reparation.

March 19, 1939, letter concerns *First Saturdays*:

> War or Peace of the world depends upon the practice of this devotion joined with the consecration to the Immaculate Heart of Mary. Hence I would want it spread, and, above all because it is the desire of our good Lord and our so dear mother in heaven... (p. 367).

Commentary

"This devotion" mentioned above refers to the *First Saturdays* devotion. This is clear from the previous paragraph in the original text not presented here. If anyone is still unsure about the "two special requests," the above words of Sr. Lucia further confirm that the consecration joined with the *First Saturdays* will bring about peace in the world. This was first proclaimed by Our Lady in her apparition on July 13, 1917.

Also, the only time the word "spread" is mentioned in the entire Fatima message is in relation to the *First Saturdays*. On December 10, 1925, during the first apparition after the Fatima apparitions, Our Lady asked for the spread of the *First Saturdays*. In the second apparition after Fatima, on February 15, 1926, Our Lord immediately asked about the spread of the *First Saturdays*. Lucia mentioned the need to spread the *First Saturdays* on May 26, 1935, on March 19, 1939 as quoted above, and again on June 20, 1939. It is clear that one cannot completely fulfill the Fatima message without spreading the *First Saturdays*.

Nonetheless, it seems that a problem has arisen as to the way in which people think peace will be brought about in the world. There is one opinion that peace will result when the Holy Father defines the dogma of the Spiritual Motherhood of Our Lady. Yet, to understand this properly, we need to take into consideration what Our Lady said at Fatima. One might think that this action of the Holy Father alone can bring peace to the world, and as a result, nothing additional would be expected of the faithful. However, at Fatima, Our Lady said that both the collegial consecration and the *First Saturdays* are the way to peace in the world. The growth in practicing the *First Saturdays* devotion will be a tremendous help in obtaining the graces necessary to proclaim the dogma of Our Lady's Spiritual Motherhood. Once the dogma is proclaimed, it will greatly further promote devotion to Our Lady, which will further increase the practice of the *First Saturdays*.

Ultimately, the Gospel peace can only result from the sanctification of the faithful. The peace spoken of by Our Lady is only possible if a significant number of people are in the state of grace and growing in holiness. The *First Saturdays* can help achieve this state of grace and growth in holiness for many. One way the *First Saturdays* achieves this is by helping to remove the obstacles of injustice against Our Lady, which stand in the way of the graces she desires to distribute.

Many petitions have been sent to the Holy Father requesting that he define the dogma of Our Lady as our Spiritual Mother by her roles as Coredemptrix, Advocate, and Mediatrix of all graces. It is true that such a teaching provides another doctrinal foundation and encouragement for our devotion to Our Blessed Mother. Devotion must be rooted in the truth, not based on sentimentality or emotion. Thus, the new dogma could provide an important *condition* for bringing peace to the world and the salvation of souls. It could also serve as a *sign* that peace is imminent.

However, the immediate *cause* of peace in the world, again, lies in the sanctification of the People of God, growing in Faith, Hope, and Love; this is the task of the *First Saturdays* given by Jesus and His Mother. In the end, the fruitful reception of Jesus in the Holy Eucharist obtained through the mediation of the Immaculate Heart of Mary will transform the world. For the Eucharist is "the source and summit of the Christian life" (*Lumen Gentium*, n. 11). A well-disposed reception of the Holy Eucharist is the most important practice of the *First Saturdays*.

Yet, this is not all. Our Lady has been greatly offended by our sins, including our sins against her Spiritual Motherhood. This requires reparation to her Immaculate Heart. This is a matter of justice and mercy. We must at least try to compensate Our Lady and her Son for these sins as best we can with the help of grace. The loving reception of the Holy Eucharist is the greatest form of reparation we can make to the Immaculate Heart of Mary. In the *Communal First Saturdays*, especially, the other practices of the *First Saturdays* prepare the way for this reception of the Holy Eucharist and provide a "continuing echo thereof" in the meditation. Let us remember that the *First Saturdays,* and in particular the *Communal First Saturdays*, is meant to enrich every day of our lives, and can provide a model for our spiritual life for every day of the month.

June 20, 1939, letter concerns *First Saturdays*, and leaflet on five *First Saturdays*. Also, Sr. Lucia said:

> Our Lady promised to restrain the scourge of War if this devotion were spread and practiced. We will see Her warding off this chastisement in the measure people will take the pain to spread the devotion, although I am afraid we are not doing as much as we could and God, not too happy, might raise His arm of Mercy and let the world be destroyed by this punishment, which as never been before shall be, *horrible, horrible.* (*Documents of Fatima and the Memoirs of Sister Lucia,* Martins and Fox, 2002, p.

368)

Commentary

While the war with actual gunfire was imminent when the above letter was written, what is said here can apply to other evils in the world as well. The question could be: how much must the *First Saturdays* be practiced to restrain war in the world? The answer given is that Our Lady wards off "chastisement in the measure people will take the pain to spread the devotion," namely, the *First Saturdays*. Sr. Lucia refers to spreading the *First Saturdays*. No doubt we can understand spreading as also meaning that more people will practice the devotion. Sr. Lucia is concerned that "we are not doing" enough to spread the devotion. It is most important to realize that the *First Saturdays* devotion is the only practice in the Fatima message that Our Lord and His Mother said to spread. Spreading the *First Saturdays* is part of the Fatima message. If we are not spreading the *First Saturdays*, we are not fully practicing the Fatima message.

In any case, the question as to how much the *First Saturdays* must be practiced to restrain war may be related to the answer to the question, how much must the *First Saturdays* be practiced to bring about peace in the world? We can say that the state of the world's tranquility seems proportionate to the effort to spread the *First Saturdays*. Again, the sufficient number of the faithful spreading and practicing the *First Saturdays* required to help bring peace to the world is known to God and not to us on earth. It would be safe to say that there will be true peace when there is a sufficient number of *First Saturdays* being fulfilled with the attempt to make reparation for the sins of the world. Nonetheless, if we are not practicing *and* spreading the *First Saturdays,* we are not fully practicing the Fatima message.

July 31, 1939, letter concerns the *First Saturdays*, and printing pamphlets about the *First Saturdays*. Sr. Lucia received a copy of the unpublished leaflet from the Bishop. The Bishop was ill but hoped to spread the *First Saturdays* devotion.

December 3, 1939, letter concerns the *First Saturdays*. Sr. Lucia did not want her name used. Sr. Lucia wrote about the publication of the five *First Saturdays* devotion by the Bishop (On September 13, 1939, the Bishop of Fatima approved the five *First Saturdays* devotion, issuing a pamphlet on the devotion with his *imprimatur*). Also, Lucia understood that Our Lady's request for the meditation on the Mysteries of the Rosary in Our Lady's company was to be fulfilled separately from the Rosary said using beads. It should also be noted that the meditation is in addition to the meditation during the Rosary said using beads.

March 19, 1940, Sr. Lucia wrote:

> In another communication, about March 1939, Our Lord said to me once more: "Ask, ask again insistently for the publication of the Communion of Reparation in honour of the Immaculate Heart of Mary on the First Saturdays. The time is coming when the rigour of my justice will punish the crimes of diverse nations. Some of them will be annihilated. At last the severity of my justice will fall severely on those who want to destroy my reign in souls" (*Memorias e Cartas da Irma Lucia*, Antonio Maria Martins, S.J., p. 465).

December 2, 1940, letter to Pope Pius XII. Sr. Lucia explained the *First Saturdays* and asked the Pope to bless and extend the devotion throughout the world. Also, Sr. Lucia asked the Pope, together with the Bishops of the world, to consecrate the world with a special mention of Russia to the Immaculate Heart of Mary.

Commentary

So, here, we begin to see the shift from merely consecrating Russia to consecrating the whole world, which had been and still is exposed to Communist errors. Russia continued to spread these errors until Gorbachev came to lead the Soviet Union, including Russia, in 1985. The collegial consecration was already having its effect through human instruments. The total collapse of Communism in the Soviet Union occurred in 1991.

Our Lord had also appeared to an extraordinary Fatima devotee in 1935, Blessed Alexandrina, and asked her to plea for the consecration of the world to the Immaculate Heart of Mary. No specific mention was made of the consecration of Russia.

Also, Sr. Lucia requested Pope Pius XII to make the consecration and to approve and recommend the *First Saturdays*. It could be interpreted that Sr. Lucia intended that the *First Saturdays* would be recommended after the persecution had stopped in Russia (cf. May 29, 1930).

March 2, 1945, Sr. Lucia was delighted with the progress of the *First Saturdays* "all over the place." Also, Sr. Lucia said the *First Saturdays* "is going to be what will save us at the present time" (*Documents of Fatima and the Memoirs of Sister Lucia,* Martins and Fox, 2002, p. 456).

Commentary

At some point in time, we could say that the *First Saturdays* became more widely known throughout the world, but since that time, it had become more of a fading memory and seemed not to be regarded as being that significant to a large number of the faithful. Even when the *First Saturdays* devotion was better regarded, there is little or no evidence that it was practiced as Our Lady requested, except possibly by very small numbers. However, there are many signs that a revival of the *First Saturdays* is now taking place.

Nonetheless, Sr. Lucia considered that the *First Saturdays* devotion was going to be effective at that time (1945) in saving them. The war ended shortly after she wrote the letter. Victory in Europe took place on May 8, 1945, and victory in Japan took place on August 15, 1945. Both victories took place on feasts of Our Lady. Much more, the *First Saturdays* devotion is sure to help save us in the time to come. Further, the *Communal First Saturdays* will help to make it easier for each individual and for a larger number of people to fulfill the *First Saturdays* request while giving visible witness to what Our Lord has done through His Mother.

Summary of the Practices of the Fatima Message

- **Repent** *("Penance, Penance, Penance!")*. (cf. penance, *CCC*, 1430-1439)

- *With love, offer* **prayers** *(including the daily Rosary and Fatima prayers) and* **sacrifices** *(including ourselves, our daily duties, and our sufferings) in supplication for the conversion of sinners and in reparation to the Sacred Heart of Jesus and the Immaculate Heart of Mary.*

- *Devotion to the* **Immaculate Heart of Mary**, *and through her, to the* **Sacred Heart of Jesus**:

  o *Make a* **consecration** *to the Immaculate Heart of Mary and wear the Brown Scapular as a sign of this consecration.*

  o *Practice* **reparation** *to the Immaculate Heart of Mary through the First Saturdays devotion and daily.*

  o *Practice* **imitation** *of the virtues of the Immaculate Heart of Mary.*

  o *Spread the First Saturdays Devotion.*

Conditions of the First Saturdays

In order to fulfill Our Lady's request for the *First Saturdays* on five consecutive first Saturdays or even more, the following 4 separate practices must each be completed **with the intention of making reparation to the Immaculate Heart of Mary:**

1. Go to **Confession** (the Sacrament of Penance or Reconciliation) * *with the intention of making reparation to the Immaculate Heart of Mary* (within 20 days).

2. Receive **Holy Communion** *with the intention of making reparation to the Immaculate Heart of Mary.*

3. Pray the **Rosary** (5 decades) *with the intention of making reparation to the Immaculate Heart of Mary.*

4. **Keep Our Lady company** for a quarter of an hour (15-minutes) while **meditating** on the Mysteries of the Rosary *with the intention of*

making reparation to the Immaculate Heart of Mary.

*One can go to Confession anytime as long as there is one Confession for each First Saturday, and as Jesus said, "as long as you receive Me in the state of grace and have the intention of making reparation to the Immaculate Heart of Mary."

The Communal First Saturdays

We have already remarked on the power of prayer in the public and communal form of the *First Saturdays*. The *Communal First Saturdays* is the only canonically approved *First Saturdays* devotion for public practice. This public devotion includes the practices of the *First Saturdays* accompanying the Liturgy so that the entire devotion may be practiced in a single period of time. In addition, there is a devotional that can be used to follow along in book form or in an app.

The Communal First Saturdays Devotional book or app provides material for examination of one's conscience, before Confession and before the devotion begins, or can be used on another day. One goes to Confession with the intention of making reparation to the Immaculate Heart of Mary.

The devotion begins with a reading of the apparition in which Our Lord and His Mother ask for the *First Saturdays*. This reminds us of what we must do to fulfill the *First Saturdays*. The intention of reparation to the Immaculate Heart of Mary and other related intentions are recited so that the purpose of the *First Saturdays* is not forgotten. We then recite the Fatima prayers, which the children repeated on a daily basis and often each day. These prayers greatly helped them to become saints and can help us as well. Other helpful prayers are then recited such as an act of consecration and an act of reparation followed by a special prayer to St. Joseph.

There follows a second practice of the *First Saturdays*, the Holy Rosary in reparation to the Immaculate Heart of Mary. This is no ordinary Rosary. This Rosary reflects the fact that at Fatima, Our Lady joined the Rosary and devotion to the Immaculate Heart of Mary together. We contemplate the Heart of Mary, especially her Love, leading us to the Heart of Jesus in the midst of the Mysteries.

The result is a combination of the power of each of these devotions. This arms the faithful with a double-powered Rosary, a double-edged sword to help defeat the kingdom of Satan. This is not all. Scripture is also added at the beginning of each decade, and the fruit of each Mystery is added as St. John Paul II recommended. This fruit or virtue is attached to the prayer that Our Lady asked us to say at the end of each decade. In sum, we are able to enter into spiritual warfare with the most advanced weapon.

St. Paul VI said the Rosary can be "an excellent preparation for the…liturgical action and…a continuing echo thereof" (*Marialis Cultus*). Let us first consider the Rosary as a preparation. If we are in the state of grace, the Rosary also disposes us to join in the offering of the Sacrifice of the Mass and receive Holy Communion. The amount of grace we receive from Jesus in Holy Communion depends on how well we are disposed. Yet, the Rosary makes us more disposed. Hence, the Rosary can serve its highest meaning as a devotion by preparing us for Jesus in the Holy Eucharist.

It should be clear that the Mass follows the common recitation of the Rosary. After joining in the offering of the Sacrifice of the Mass, we arrive at the third practice of the *First Saturdays*. Hence, we are able to offer a Communion of Reparation for the sins against the Immaculate Heart of Mary. Unrepaired sins block the flow of grace from Jesus through Mary and from Mary through the Church into the world. It is important to remember that any reparation to the Heart of Mary primarily makes reparation to the Heart of Jesus, Who has given us the Heart of His Mother.

The Mass is followed by the 15-minute meditation requested by Our Lady in reparation to her Immaculate Heart. In the *Catechism of the Catholic Church*, in the section on meditation, only two forms of meditation are mentioned, *lectio divina* and the Rosary (n. 2708). Hence, to fulfill Our Lady's request, we keep Our Lady company for 15-minutes while meditating on the Mysteries of the Rosary by using that ancient form of meditation, the *lectio divina*. The *lectio divina* allows us to meditate on the very words of Scripture from which the Mysteries of the Rosary are derived. St. Jerome said that "ignorance of Scripture is ignorance of Christ." It could also be said that ignorance of Scripture is ignorance of the Rosary. This is one reason why St. John Paul II promoted the use of Scripture while the faithful say the Rosary.

We can be sure that the use of the *lectio divina* for the meditation will help to strengthen our recitation of the Rosary in the ordinary form. Further, while the Holy Eucharist is still within us, the Scriptural meditation can help us to receive the continual flow of grace from the Lamb of God in greater measure.

At the end of the *Communal First Saturdays*, it is recommended that the Pilgrim Virgin Statue Church to Home Visitation be added. Instead of going from church to church or home to home, the Pilgrim Virgin travels from the church after Mass to the home to enthrone the Sacred Heart of Jesus, bring the Fatima message, and promote the family Rosary. On the following Saturday or First Saturday, the family brings the Pilgrim Virgin back to the church before Mass. This visitation enables the *Communal First Saturdays* to reach into the homes of the faithful, to greatly help the needs of the family, and then return the family to Jesus in the Holy Eucharist.

Also, Jesus told Sr. Lucia in 1930 that one of the five reasons for five *First Saturdays* is to make reparation for the offenses against Our Lady's images. The *Pilgrim Virgin Statue Church to Home Visitation*, as a part of the *Communal First Saturdays,* is a wonderful enhancement of our gift of reparation.

Following the reception of the Pilgrim Virgin statue, the Brown Scapular of Our Lady of Mt. Carmel may be received by those who so desire. The Brown Scapular may be worn as a sign of consecration to the Immaculate Heart of Mary. Further, Sr. Lucia said that it is inseparable from the Rosary. Also, the tradition states that those who die wearing it, will not suffer the loss of their soul. This means that those who so honor Our Lady will be given the graces to repent before death.

One could say that the *Communal First Saturdays* is a kind of microcosm of the entire Fatima message, centered around the Lamb of God, and Who is approached through the Immaculate Heart of Mary. It is a kind of little retreat, and a school of holiness that can change one's life.

The *First Saturdays* is a devotion that we must continue to practice, in order to obtain a peace that is only possible when all nations have embraced the Catholic Faith and have formed a Catholic culture. We know that the fulfillment of the *First Saturdays* is essential to that reparation to the Immaculate Heart of Mary that will clear the way for peace and the spiritual reign of the Lamb of God. Yet, Our Lady must be honored for bringing about such a great triumph.

Yet, who would know if we merely fulfill the *First Saturdays* privately? Public and communal prayer is most efficacious. The public and communal practice of the *First Saturdays,* especially the *Communal First Saturdays*, in parishes throughout the world will bear witness, without question, that the triumph has been achieved through the Immaculate Heart of Mary. What a joy it will be for each of us to have participated in this triumph by practicing and spreading this devotion.

Outline of a Model Communal First Saturdays

Each of the following is offered in reparation to the Immaculate Heart of Mary

-1:00 **Individual Confessions** (Sacrament of Penance or Reconciliation)
-0:40 Communal devotion begins with intentions and prayers
-0:30 **The Rosary**
 0:00 **The Holy Sacrifice of the Mass** with the **Communion of Reparation**
 0:30 **Scripture Meditation** on the Mysteries of the Rosary while keeping Our Lady company (in a communal form of *lectio divina*)
 0:50 Litany and Prayers for the Holy Father
 0:55 Reception of the Pilgrim Virgin Statue in the Church
 1:00 Reception of the Brown Scapular

0:00 represents whatever the actual starting time for the Holy Mass is in the particular parish or community. Thus, the Rosary begins 30 minutes before the starting time for the Holy Mass, the intentions and prayers begin 40 minutes before the start of the Holy Mass, and the *lectio divina* meditation with Scripture begins after the conclusion of the Holy Mass (about 30 minutes after the starting time for the Holy Mass). The Litany of the Blessed Virgin Mary and prayers for the Holy Father follow.

Other recommended devotions, such as the *Pilgrim Virgin Statue Church to Home Visitation*, would begin after the litany and prayers for the Holy Father (about 55 minutes after the starting time for the Holy Mass). Otherwise, the *Communal First Saturdays* would close at that time. If there is the Reception of the Brown Scapular of Our Lady of Mt. Carmel, it would take place last, either after the reception of the Pilgrim Virgin Statue or after the Prayers for the Holy Father. If possible, individual Confessions would begin an hour or more before the Holy Mass. One would need to check the parish schedule for actual times. All times are approximate.

Also, it is important to keep in mind that to fully practice the Fatima Message, we need to spread the *First Saturdays*. Please see www.CommunalFirstSaturdays.org. There one will find more information about the *Communal First Saturdays* and useful materials for spreading this devotion. These materials include *The Communal First Saturdays Devotional,* which can be passed out and collected on the *First Saturdays*. For more information about starting the *Communal First Saturdays* in the parish, please contact us at info@CommunalFirstSaturdays.org.

Appendix

Fatima Prayers and How to Say the Rosary

Fatima Prayers

My God, I believe, I adore, I hope, and I love You; I ask pardon of You for those who do not believe, do not adore, do not hope, and do not love You.

Most Holy Trinity, Father, Son, and Holy Spirit I adore You profoundly. I offer You the Most Precious Body, Blood, Soul, and Divinity of Jesus Christ, present in all the tabernacles throughout the world, in reparation for the outrages, sacrileges, and indifference by which He is offended. And through the infinite merits of His most Sacred Heart, and of the Immaculate Heart of Mary, I beg the conversion of poor sinners.

O Most Holy Trinity, I adore You. My God, my God, I love You in the most Blessed Sacrament.

O Jesus, this is for love of You, for the conversion of sinners, for the Holy Father, and in reparation for the sins committed against the Immaculate Heart of Mary. *(Jacinta added "the Holy Father.")*

O my Jesus, forgive us our sins, save us from the fires of hell; lead all souls to Heaven, especially those in most need of Thy mercy.

Sweet Heart of Mary be my salvation!

The first two prayers were taught by the Angel of Peace to the children of Fatima (Lucia, Francisco, and Jacinta). The third prayer was inspired within the children by an inner impulse of the Holy Spirit, and the next two were taught to them by Our Lady of the Rosary. Our Lady requested that the fifth prayer be said at the end of each decade of the Rosary. Here we retain the popular form. Jacinta was inspired to say the last prayer, "Sweet Heart of Mary..."

How to Pray the Rosary

This section called "How to pray the Rosary" is to help those individuals unfamiliar with saying the Rosary. One of the elements of the Rosary is the contemplation of the Mysteries "in communion with Mary" (cf. St. Paul VI, Marialis Cultus, n. 49).

The Rosary is ordinarily said in the following manner.

Begin by making the Sign of the Cross.

In the name of the Father, and of the Son, and of the Holy Spirit.

Using Rosary beads, pray the Apostles' Creed holding the Crucifix:

I believe in God, the Father almighty, Creator of heaven and earth, and in Jesus Christ, his only Son, our Lord, who was conceived by the Holy Spirit, born of the Virgin Mary, suffered under Pontius Pilate, was crucified, died and was buried; he descended into hell; on the third day he rose again from the dead; he ascended into heaven, and is seated at the right hand of God the Father almighty; from there he will come to judge the living and the dead.

I believe in the Holy Spirit, the holy catholic Church, the communion of saints, the forgiveness of sins, the resurrection of the body, and life everlasting. Amen.

On the large bead, pray the Our Father (the Lord's Prayer):

Our Father, who art in heaven, hallowed be thy name; thy kingdom come, thy will be done on earth, as it is in heaven. Give us this day, our daily bread, and forgive us our trespasses, as we forgive those who trespass against us; and lead us not into temptation, but deliver us from evil. Amen.

On the next three small beads, pray the Hail Mary:

Hail Mary full of grace, the Lord is with thee; blessed art thou among women, and blessed is the Fruit of thy womb, Jesus. Holy Mary, Mother of God, pray for us sinners now, and at the hour of our death. Amen.

Then pray the Glory Be:

Glory be to the Father, and to the Son, and to the Holy Spirit, as it was in the beginning, is now, and ever shall be, world without end. Amen.

The Mysteries of the Rosary chosen may correspond to the day of the week. Ordinarily, the Mysteries that may be chosen are as follows:

- *The Joyful Mysteries on Mondays and Saturdays.*
- *The Luminous Mysteries on Thursdays.*
- *The Sorrowful Mysteries on Tuesdays and Fridays.*
- *The Glorious Mysteries on Wednesdays and Sundays.*

Announce or call to mind the mystery before each decade. Calling to mind a related Scripture verse or two is recommended by St. John Paul II before each decade (Rosarium Virginis Mariae).

The Joyful Mysteries

The First Joyful Mystery: The Annunciation of the Lord
The Second Joyful Mystery: The Visitation of Mary to Elizabeth
The Third Joyful Mystery: The Birth of Jesus
The Fourth Joyful Mystery: The Presentation of the Child Jesus in the Temple
The Fifth Joyful Mystery: The Finding of the Child Jesus in the Temple

The Luminous Mysteries

The First Luminous Mystery: The Baptism of Our Lord
The Second Luminous Mystery: The Marriage Feast at Cana
The Third Luminous Mystery: The Proclamation of the Gospel
The Fourth Luminous Mystery: The Transfiguration of Jesus Christ
The Fifth Luminous Mystery: The Institution of the Holy Eucharist

The Sorrowful Mysteries

The First Sorrowful Mystery: The Agony of Jesus in the Garden
The Second Sorrowful Mystery: The Scourging of Jesus at the Pillar
The Third Sorrowful Mystery: The Crowning of Jesus with Thorns
The Fourth Sorrowful Mystery: Jesus Carries the Cross

The Fifth Sorrowful Mystery: The Crucifixion and Death of Our Lord

The Glorious Mysteries

The First Glorious Mystery: The Resurrection of Jesus from the Dead

The Second Glorious Mystery: The Ascension of Jesus into Heaven

The Third Glorious Mystery: The Descent of the Holy Spirit upon Mary and the Apostles

The Fourth Glorious Mystery: The Assumption of Mary into Heaven

The Fifth Glorious Mystery: The Crowning of Mary as Queen of Heaven and Earth

On the large bead, pray the Our Father.

On the ten small beads, pray the Hail Mary.

At the end of each decade, pray the Glory Be.

Each decade is followed by the Fatima prayer requested by Our Lady:

O my Jesus, forgive us our sins, save us from the fires of hell; lead all souls to Heaven, especially those in most need of Thy mercy.

Although one is not required to say the above prayer in order to say the Rosary, we recommend the use of this prayer because Our Lady taught the children of Fatima to say this prayer. Our Lady requested that this prayer be said at the end of each decade of the Rosary. Our Lady made this request on July 13, 1917, the same day she spoke of the First Saturdays.

The following is another version of the prayer that might be preferred: "O my Jesus, forgive us, save us from the fire of hell. Lead all souls to Heaven, especially those who are most in need" ("Fatima in Lucia's own words," Dominican Nuns of Perpetual Rosary, p. 179). This is a literal translation from Lucia's own words. Local usage may vary from this translation while sufficiently retaining the original meaning. Thus the popular form may be retained in order to avoid any confusion.

At the end of the five decades, say the Hail Holy Queen.

Hail Holy Queen, Mother of mercy, our life, our sweetness and our hope. To thee do we cry, poor banished children of Eve. To thee do we send up our sighs, mourning and weeping in this vale of tears. Turn then most gracious advocate, thine eyes of mercy towards us, and after this our exile, show unto us the blessed fruit of thy womb, Jesus. O clement, O loving, O sweet Virgin Mary. Pray for us, O holy Mother of God. That we may be made worthy of the promises of Christ.

Let us pray

O God, whose only begotten Son, by His Life, Death, and Resurrection, has purchased for us the rewards of eternal life, grant we beseech thee, that meditating on these Mysteries of the Most Holy Rosary of the Blessed Virgin Mary, we may imitate what they contain, and obtain what they promise, through the same Christ Our Lord. Amen.

Contact Information

For more information or questions, please contact:
Communal First Saturdays Apostolate
www.CommunalFirstSaturdays.org
Email:
info@communalfirstsaturdays.org